The Incredible Flexible You™

A Social Thinking® Curriculum for the Preschool and Early Elementary Years

Ryan Hendrix | Kari Zweber Palmer | Nancy Tarshis | Michelle Garcia Winner

SocialThinking.com®

Social Thinking Publishing, San Jose, CA

www.socialthinking.com

W9-DGX-019

The Incredible Flexible You

A Social Thinking Curriculum for the Preschool and Early Elementary Years

Ryan Hendrix, Kari Zweber Palmer, Nancy Tarshis and Michelle Garcia Winner

Library of Congress Control Number: 2013930268

Volume 1 ISBN: 978-1-9369430-5-0
Curriculum ISBN: 978-1-9369430-6-7

Social Developmental Timeline images from iStockphoto.com contributors: tuncaycetin, Gelpi, jall-free, jfairone, pawelwizja, hidesy, and aabejon. Background cover image: iStockphoto.com/kentarca-juan.

Social Thinking Publishing
3031 Tisch Way, Suite 800
San Jose, CA 95128
Phone: (877) 464-9278
Fax: (408) 557-8594

This book is printed and bound in Tennessee by Mighty Color Printing
Books may be ordered online at www.socialthinking.com

Praise for
The Incredible Flexible You

A Social Thinking Curriculum for the Preschool and Early Elementary Years

"Here is a much needed, creative and engaging curriculum for our youngest learners with social thinking challenges. As a special education teacher, I have found it challenging to teach the basics of Social Thinking to young children. *The Incredible Flexible You* provides lessons, literature, and ideas to expand the teachings of Michelle Garcia Winner. Supported by research about how children learn the complexities of the social world, the authors provide rich and well-defined curricula, which professionals can use to help our earliest learners become better social thinkers."

–D.M., Special education teacher

"*The Incredible Flexible You* provides the missing curriculum we have all been searching for to teach Social Thinking concepts to children in preschool and early elementary school. This curriculum is effective for all children and is especially beneficial to children with high functioning autism. Our early childhood special education program had the privilege of working with co-author Kari Palmer to pilot lessons from *The Incredible Flexible You* in our inclusion program. We saw phenomenal results! The curriculum is easy to use, has a clear scope and sequence for teaching essential Social Thinking concepts for school success, and has practical ideas for families to use at home. I cannot recommend this book highly enough!"

– M.S., Autism specialist

"My son has been learning various Social Thinking Vocabulary and concepts from therapists over the past 4.5 years, but these concepts were scattered and he didn't really 'connect the dots' until he learned how they all come together in the 'group plan.' These basic, yet important building blocks are covered comprehensively and taught methodically in this curriculum. Highly recommended for anyone who is interested in learning Social Thinking."

– S.T., Parent

"As a speech language pathologist in the inclusive preschool setting, I have witnessed exciting changes in the social emotional skills of our preschool children after using *The Incredible Flexible You* curriculum and stories. The children have been excited to learn about each new adventure taken by Evan, Ellie, Jesse and Molly and to then participate in the related activities in their own classroom. The concrete stories and activities provide an integrated way to teach the Social Thinking Vocabulary to students. Plus, I found the hands-on curriculum gave me the means to obtain a greater understanding of this curriculum, which in turn, allowed me to create my own activities."

–K.H., Speech language pathologist

"The Incredible Flexible You series has brought excitement to the process of learning Social Thinking in our preschool-aged children. The easy-to-use stories and engaging large and small group activities have been a wonderful learning opportunity for my teaching team and eager students. The stories took each child on adventures from the heights of space, to deep shark infested caves. I would suggest this series for any teacher helping children grow in social thinking skills and concepts!"

–P.J., Teacher

"As an early childhood special education teacher, I have found *The Incredible Flexible You* curriculum to offer a clear map on how to introduce various Social Thinking concepts in a fun and engaging way. It includes a variety of invaluable tools that help with planning instructional activities. The storybooks and lessons have enabled me to provide a strong foundation for social-emotional development in *all* children in our classroom as it not only benefits children with social-emotional delays, but also community peers.

Our students are using vocabulary from the curriculum and are doing so in appropriate ways that exhibit a true understanding of the Social Thinking concepts across settings and social contexts. To follow are a few quotes from our students:

Teacher Courtney, did I change your thoughts?
(Following a short discussion about a behavior problem during learning centers.)

I'm going to think with my eyes to choose a friend.
(During Show and Tell; his peers then waited for him to look at them before asking their question.)

Please stop. That makes me have unexpected thoughts!
(During a conflict with a peer during playtime.)

Stop talking and put your brain back in the group.
(During circle time when a peer was not attending.)"

–C.B., Early childhood special education teacher

The Incredible Flexible You™ Music CD

What makes any classroom, any lesson, or any learning experience more memorable, more enjoyable, and more fun?

Music.

In this new curriculum, the powerful ideas and strategies of Social Thinking have been adapted to preschool and early elementary youngsters. Even better, they've been put to music. And not by just anyone.

The Incredible Flexible You CD features 12 new songs written by award-winning songwriters Phil Galdston and Tom Chapin, and performed by "The Pied Piper of Children's Music," three-time GRAMMY® winner Tom Chapin.

The songs were written to accompany the storybooks, making the lessons so much easier to teach and that much more fun to learn. They also stand alone as catchy, singable, kid-friendly, and adult-safe tunes to play in the classroom, in the home, or even in the family car.

Tom Chapin

Through 40 years, 22 CDs, eight GRAMMY nominations, three GRAMMY awards, and thousands of live performances, Tom Chapin has entertained, amused and enlightened audiences of all ages. A pioneer in the field of children's music, he is also a respected singer/songwriter and powerful advocate for the Arts in Education. *Billboard Magazine* calls him, "The best family artist around," and *The New York Times,* "One of the great personalities in contemporary folk music." In his varied career,

Chapin has appeared on Broadway as Jim in the hit musical *Pump Boys and Dinettes* and off-Broadway as musical director of *Cotton Patch Gospel* and *Harry Chapin: Lies & Legends.* In film, he created the music for the award-winning shark documentary *Blue Water, White Death* and had a cameo role as Vice President Edward Nelson in the 2004 remake of *The Manchurian Candidate.* On television Chapin hosted the ABC Emmy & Peabody award-winning children's show *Make A Wish* and the documentary series *National Geographic Explorer.* He is a contributor to National Public Radio's *Morning Edition,* creating and performing topical songs poking fun at social and scientific trends in the news. For more information about Chapin visit www.tomchapin.com.

Phil Galdston

Phil Galdston is a songwriter/producer whose work has appeared on nearly 70 million records and on the soundtracks of numerous films and TV programs. His words and music have graced recordings by such artists as Yolanda Adams, America, Beyoncé, Brandy, Celine Dion, Cher, Chicago, Marc Cohn, Sheryl Crow, Kurt Elling, Aaron Neville, Esperanza Spalding, and Vanessa Williams, who has recorded many of his songs, including "Save the Best For Last." Phil has received the Grand Prize of the American Song Festival, four ASCAP awards, the Time For Peace Award, two Nashville Songwriters' Association citations, and Cable ACE, DOVE Award, and GRAMMY nominations. Overall, his work has been featured on 14 GRAMMY-nominated or winning records. Phil was recently appointed the first member of the Songwriting Faculty and the first Faculty Songwriter-in-Residence in New York University's history. He is the founder, curator, and moderator of the Songwriters Hall of Fame Master Sessions at NYU.

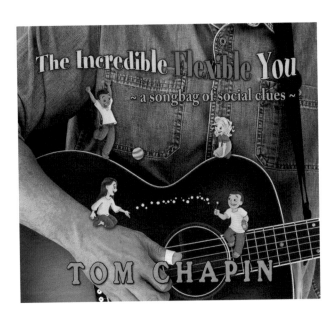

Look for the accompanying CD at socialthinking.com and tomchapin.com.

Dedication

We dedicate this with love

to the incredibly flexible people in our lives

who have supported and inspired this work.

Tres and Kyle Hendrix,

Ellie and Erik Mogalian,

Jane and Joe Zweber,

Evan, Nora and Ryan Palmer,

Maya Gomes,

Molly, Jesse and Phil Galdston,

Suzette and Sy Tarshis.

Acknowledgments

This project was inspired by requests from the Social Thinking community, families, and professionals looking for a way to bring these powerful concepts to our youngest learners.

Ryan, Kari, and Nancy wish to acknowledge that the book series and curriculum are profoundly indebted to the concepts and ground-breaking work of Michelle Garcia Winner, without whose teaching, guidance, and support this would not have been possible.

Ryan, Kari, Nancy and Michelle are eternally grateful to our many friends, family, and colleagues who listened to ideas, looked at sketches, sang along to the music, asked questions, and, on occasion, got out their red pens.

Special thanks to Pam Crooke, whose keen eye, level head, and supreme problem-solving abilities were essential to completing the project. Additional thanks go to our editor, Veronica Zysk, and art director, Elizabeth Blacker, for their vision and for keeping us on track.

Thanks, also, to the families and professionals who were part of the development and early drafts, exploring social learning with our main characters in their Crayola® marker form and using the activities in their groups and classrooms. We thank:

The staff and families at Social Thinking Stevens Creek; the staff and families of the Rainbow Room; Minnetonka Preschool; the staff and families of the Eden Prairie early childhood special education program; the staff and families of the Children's Evaluation and Rehabilitation Center at Einstein College of Medicine; and Debbie Meringolo and Altogether Social.

Finally, to the many families with whom we work: thank you for the honor and privilege of sharing this journey. We're all always learning from and with you.

Contents

Introduction 1
    What is Social Thinking? 2
    How does Social Thinking Emerge in Typically Developing Children? 3
    When Social Development Goes Awry: What is a Social Learning Challenge? .. 15
    Why Teach Social Thinking in Preschool and Early Elementary? 22
    Social Thinking Vocabulary for the Preschool and Early Elementary Years 24
    Interpreting Difficult Behavior Through the Lens of Social Thinking 33

Curriculum Overview 36
    Target Ages and Population 36
    Grouping 37
    How to Use the Book 37
    Assessing Your Students' Progress 39
    Ideas for Writing Goals 40
    Using The Incredible Flexible You Music CD 40

Lesson Layout 41
    Opening Routine 41
    Introduce the Vocabulary using The Incredible Flexible You Storybooks 44
    Closing Routine 47
    Beyond the Lesson: Generalize the Vocabulary to Other Settings 48
    Take Away Points for the Lesson 48
    The Family Letter: Extending Learning Outside the Classroom 48

Lesson 1. Thinking Thoughts and Feeling Feelings 49
Lesson 2. The Group Plan 71
Lesson 3. Thinking With Your Eyes 89
Lesson 4. Body in the Group 109
Lesson 5. Whole Body Listening 125

Appendix A. Templates 143
Appendix B. Song Lyrics 159
Appendix C. Family Letters 171
Appendix D. Ideas for Goal Writing 183

Bibliography 189

About the Authors 193

CD Contents

Diagram 1. Building Blocks of Typical Preschool Social Development
Diagram 2. The Shaky Foundation When Social Development Goes Awry
Diagram 3. Social Thinking as a Supportive Framework
Social Developmental Timeline

Teaching Moments

Appendix A. Templates
Appendix B. Song Lyrics
Appendix C. Family Letters
Appendix D. Ideas for Goal Writing

Introduction

One day in the housekeeping corner in a preschool classroom, five four-year-olds—Thomas, Esther, Alison, Angel, and Enrique – were playing in a group. Having already decided they would be a family, they divided up the roles and play began. Thomas and Esther (the parents) busied themselves organizing and setting up the kitchen with a set of plastic dishes and food, Alison and Enrique (the older and younger siblings) were playing with blocks and Angel (the baby) was taking a nap. Alison and Enrique play out an argument that Thomas comes in to referee, sending each child to their own corner for a time out. Esther continues in the kitchen, setting the table for five and moving plastic food from pot to plate. Meanwhile, Angel wakes up and calls out, "I wanna come out and play." Immediately all four children turn in his direction, with annoyed looks on their faces. Confused, Angel says, "What did I do?" Thomas wags a finger and admonishes him, "You can't talk; you're the baby."

In this short vignette, we can see the many important facets of development that underlie skilled play in pre-school children. What looks like pure fun to us has important social consequences for developing minds. The ability to participate in collaborative pretend play depends upon flexible thinking, sufficient language ability, the capacity for abstract thought, self-regulation, solid social-emotional development and perspective taking, as well as the executive function skills needed to understand the context of the play sequence and the multi-tasking involved. As you read ahead, keep in mind the complexity of the social landscape and the speed with which typical children process and respond to this vital, and rapidly changing, information.

The Incredible Flexible You™ curriculum is designed to help young learners with average to way above average language and learning ability develop the skills they need to be flexible social thinkers and social problem solvers. We do this by teaching Michelle Garcia Winner's Social Thinking® concepts and vocabulary at the preschool and young elementary level. Because Social Thinking is a thought-based approach, explicitly taught through describing and demonstrating concrete concepts through structured play, it is best utilized with students who have the capacity to learn through language. Students will learn about the social mind, social expectations, their own thinking and that of others, to help them make better decisions when in the midst of social play and interaction. *Better yet,* teachers and caregivers will learn how to explain these abstract concepts to them!

The curriculum is taught through the experiences of four children, Evan, Ellie, Jesse, and Molly, as they go through various adventures presented in storybook format. Ten lessons align with the ten storybooks that are part of this teaching series. Volume 1 introduces five stories and their accompanying curriculum lessons; Volume 2 includes the remaining five storybooks and lessons. Each lesson is designed to teach a specific Social Thinking concept via one of the vocabulary terms. Once a concept is introduced, it is then used across all other lessons during relevant moments. The vocabulary builds upon itself; the ideas are not discreet session to session. Social learning takes time; it is not expected for students to learn a concept after one lesson. Instead, increasingly higher levels of understanding evolve across the use of the curriculum and especially when the Social Thinking Vocabulary is explored beyond the lesson and across the day through *The Incredible Flexible You* music CD and the at-home activities teachers can share with parents and families.

What is Social Thinking?

Social Thinking = ME + YOU = US

It is really as simple, and as complex, as that. It is the complicated mental math we do to combine our understanding of the situation, our collective social expectations which then relate to our thoughts, the thoughts of others, our behaviors, the behaviors of others, and all the attendant reactions into every *human* interaction. Being a good social thinker means we appreciate how we "fit" into the world with others and how others fit into our own interior world. We can take what we see, what we hear and what we feel about others or a situation and filter it through what we already think, feel, and know to make smart guesses about what is happening around us. We can take into account who we are, where we are, who we are with, and flexibly adapt in a split second. Most of the time, we don't even know we are doing it.

What we think and feel about ourselves and others drives our relationships and our interactions even during the preschool years! I think about what I think about you, you think about what you think about me, and we each think about each other's thoughts. Wanting to keep each other thinking positive thoughts and feeling good feelings is what motivates our behavior.

Typical development of social thinking encompasses far more than merely demonstrating social skills. It goes beyond understanding that different situations lend themselves to different sets of socials skills. It also includes the knowledge that we, and others, have beliefs, feelings and understandings that drive and explain our own and others' behaviors and that they are not always the same. We call this developmental concept **theory of mind**. This deep and evolving understanding of the "contents" of another person's mind and emotions enables the ability to act on that understanding to initiate and maintain an interaction, and, ultimately, a relationship. When we consider the many variables involved in any given social situation, including people, setting and past history to inform our own behavior, we're engaging in **perspective taking**. This includes making choices based on how we want others to feel and how we want them to see and treat us. This, in turn, affects how we feel and see ourselves.

For example, let's say I decide that one cookie is all my preschooler may have right now. I offer her one and, while she watches, put the rest in the tall cabinet. Later, during her nap, I realize that if I freeze the rest of the cookies, I won't have to bake for my company next weekend. Upon waking, my preschooler heads straight to the tall cabinet. "Oh, they're not there," I say. "I froze them for Grandma and Grandpa's visit. How about your favorite: peanut butter and apple?" This reminder of an upcoming happy event and offer of an acceptable substitute heads off a tantrum. Because I possess a theory of mind and can engage in perspective taking, I "read" my daughter's intention and acted accordingly, thereby averting a minor crisis and continuing our afternoon pleasantly. This is the essence of social thinking, the ability to know our own plan, read someone else's plan, and adapt as needed so that both parties remain engaged and feeling good about the experience. Social thinking is what keeps us connected to others, helps us share space effectively, think flexibly and act collaboratively. It is also what we do when we are not interacting. When we read a novel and interpret the thoughts and emotions of the characters within the context of the story, we are using social thinking. When we sit quietly in a room with another person and don't talk because we know that person is concentrating on something important, or when we mentally review the events of the day and think about what we may have done differently, we are also using our social thinking.

How does Social Thinking Emerge in Typically Developing Children?

In this chapter we will be breaking down social development into its component parts to present material in a sequence where learning can occur. (See Diagram 1.) In doing so, we want you to remember two important ideas: 1) we're talking about a whole child, and 2) development is neither completely linear nor can teaching of one aspect be considered apart from everything else happening within the child. We are dissecting for you what the social brain does naturally and synergistically within typically developing children who acquire this social radar largely without direct instruction. Yet, how neurotypical children learn information intuitively cannot be replicated when we have to teach it mechanically or cognitively, one concept at a time in a linear manner.

Cognitive and emotional developments in early childhood are intrinsically related. These synergistic facets connect to form a fully functional, fully integrated, happy, healthy, playful, and interactive preschool child. We will explore the building blocks that underlie perspective taking in children through their fourth year of life (these include the co-mingling of executive function, central coherence and theory of mind), and the Common Core Standards expected by the time they hit kindergarten. This will help us further our understanding of social development. From there, we can build our teaching model to help our preschool and early elementary school age students be increasingly successful at co-existing, working and playing as part of a larger group.

Social development starts from the minute we are born (Shonkoff & Phillips, 2000). In fact, we now know it is probably more hard-wired than we ever thought. Babies arrive with fundamental neurologically-based social capabilities, which are pruned, shaped, encouraged and developed through experiential learning and the brain's physical development. (This is referred to elsewhere as "neurological development.") Brain development, which is very rapid in the first two years of life, is enhanced by responsive caregiving and appropriate stimulation. However, under-stimulation or hard-wired neurological impediments to receiving and or perceiving stimulation shape neural function in maladaptive ways. Students born to social learning challenges are not neurologically hard-wired to acquire social information in the same developmental trajectory or speed when compared to their socially astute peers.

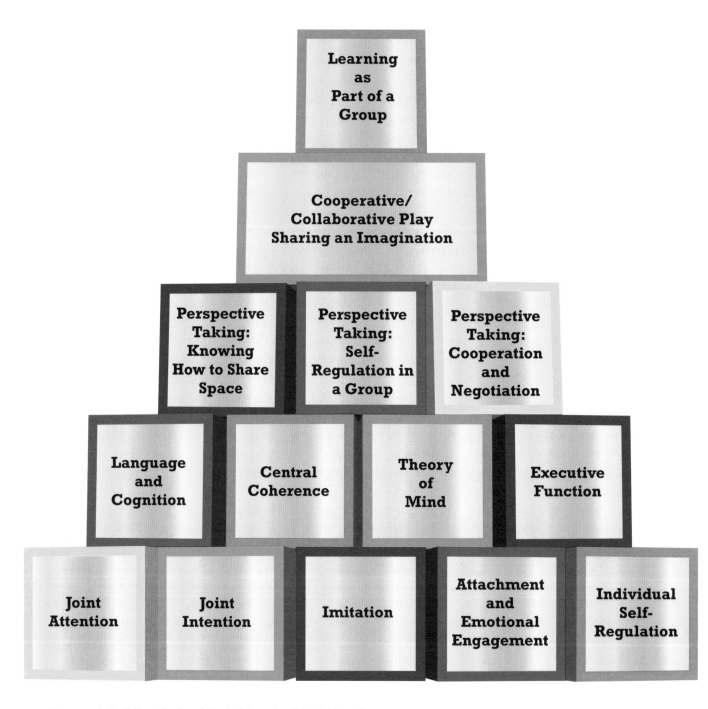

Diagram 1: Building Blocks of Typical Preschool Social Development

For the purpose of explaining the foundations of preschool social development, we have separated these fundamental capacities into separate blocks. However, please remember they are synergistic, interrelated and interdependent. You will notice they are placed in layers that climb to the pinnacle of cooperative/collaborative play and learning in a group. Each layer represents capacities that are inherently connected and interdependent as well as emerging in a similar time frame in development. One layer builds upon the next, resulting in a fully functional and flexible kindergarten-ready child, armed with the social thinking and social processing skills needed to play with others and learn in a group.

Development of Imitation and Joint Attention

Mutual engagement starts with those very first smiles between parent and child. The early development of self-regulation is based on shared emotion: babies act and react in direct response to the caregiving they receive. They know how they feel because they watch their parents' faces. They react to the stimulation parents provide and from this a sense of sharing arises (Carpenter et al., 1998).

During the early months, those first sounds give way to mutual coos and smiles, delightful to both. Baby coos, mommy smiles. Baby frowns, mom frowns. Soon, mommy tickles produce baby giggles, in a mutual song and dance of the heart. This is the beginning of social reciprocity.

Eye contact and mutual gazing can be observed as early as three to four months of age (Farroni et al., 2002). Anyone who has fed or played with a three-month-old infant is involved with the earliest form of socio-communicative interaction. Who doesn't remember falling in love with an infant while gazing into the child's face?

Baby games and baby play are all about reciprocity **and** are the underpinnings of joining attention that sow the seeds for the development of theory of mind. An example: a six–month-old baby is in a restaurant with mommy and her friend. Baby begins to fuss, so mommy shakes her keys to quiet her. Baby reaches and smiles, and peace is restored. At nine months, they find themselves in the same circumstance. Lo and behold, baby now looks intently at mommy's keys and, miraculously, mommy gives them over. She *knows* what baby wants. Finally, at 12 months, baby looks at the keys, at mommy, then back at the keys. It is a clear, yet wordless, request. You are observing the distinguishable difference between eye gaze for engagement and instrumental eye gaze designed to accomplish a goal. This is the root of social development; not only have they engaged in an act of joint attention, but they both know that they have done so! In thinking about the development of perspective taking, this "knowing," which happens just before the first birthday (Tomasello, 1995), is a crucial milestone.

Now, let's combine our heartfelt knowledge with the research. Andrew Meltzoff and his colleagues (Meltzoff, 2005) proved that imitation, the observation and then execution of behavior, is typically acquired innately. They were able to show that infants as young as *four hours old* are able to replicate tongue protrusion. Newborns also imitate facial expressions; *I see it, I do it.*

There are two important aspects going on here. Typically developing infants are born able to imitate, which helps them build a catalogue of behaviors. They develop a "social memory" and can repeat the behavior again hours later! Infants also use the behavior of others to learn about and expand their repertoire. At 14 months they begin to recognize when they are being imitated. Meltzoff and colleagues showed that infants smile more and gaze longer at adults who imitate them, indicating they are aware of the imitation.

The innate capacity for imitation is crucial. It biases children's behavior toward participation in reciprocal interactions with their caregivers and, in turn, attracts caregivers. After all, what working parent has not found it difficult to leave a wide-awake, cooing and smiling infant? In fact, because "like me" experiences are embedded within reciprocal experiences, these early exchanges with caregivers set the stage for social development that builds understanding of the intentions of others (Meltzoff, 2005). Early games, like "How big is baby?" and Peek-a-Boo teach the rhythms of conversation, as well as how to be contingent and responsive.

Being responsive to the actions and reactions of others leads to social referencing. Very early, infants learn to observe adult facial expressions for information about safety, approval, and interest. Anyone who has watched a toddler fall down on the sidewalk and look to a parent for a reaction has witnessed this in action. If the parent looks upset or offers immediate comfort, the toddler will cry as if badly injured. However, if the parent smiles and says, "You're okay," the toddler will stand up, dust off, and keep moving. Toddlers are also aware of the difference between familiar and unfamiliar adults, and when distressed, will avoid seeking out unfamiliar adults to comfort them.

> A baby is born with an imitative brain, which provides the physical structure from which social concepts can emerge and develop through social play with caregivers.

In addition to establishing social referencing and being able to imitate the behavior of others, we also know that children 12–15 months old categorize human acts in terms of intentions (Tomasello et al., 2005). If I see a behavior that is in my repertoire, I can interpret the meaning and the intention of that behavior based on my own experience. The ability to view, imitate and understand imitation underlies the capacity for theory of mind. If I have scrunched up my face in response to a bitter flavor and, then see another person do the same, I can interpret their facial expression as a reaction to bitterness because I have had the same experience. As Meltzoff (2005) described: typically developing infants interpret the acts of others with "felt" meaning because it is "like me."

Studies have shown that when adults watch others reach for and grasp objects, the same location in the brain of the watcher is activated as in the brain of the doer (Meltzoff and Decety, 2003). What's more, in subsequent research they discovered this same location in the brain was activated when adults were engaged in theory of mind tasks! This pairing suggests that imitation (and the neural network that supports it) gives rise to theory of mind. In other words, the crux of Meltzoff's *Like Me* hypothesis is that infants may use their own actions as a framework for interpreting the actions of others.

This innate matching of self to other (imitation and the recognition of being imitated) is crucial to the development of empathy, role taking, and putting yourself in someone else's place. A baby is born with an imitative brain, which provides the physical structure from which social concepts can emerge and develop through social play with caregivers. The result is the development of theory of mind and, ultimately, perspective taking.

Development of Joint Intention

The capacity for **joint attention** enables a child to develop strategies for establishing shared attention, engaging in social monitoring and social referencing, and for considering another person's perspective. The origins of joint attention appear early in infancy, with the first smiles, coos, and mutual delight shared with another human being. At six months, infants broaden their attention to include objects. This interest in toys and other playthings leads them to signal caregivers when these objects are out of reach. At nine months, they not only look in the direction of interesting objects and actions, they follow the head turn of others to see where they are looking (Meltzoff et al., 2007, 2009). At this point, it is the movement of the other person's head that drives their shift in attention. Infants will turn to look even if the adult's eyes are closed (Meltzoff et al., 2007, 2009).

Even more amazing, in just two more months they have already significantly increased their knowledge: at 10–11 months, they no longer turn to see what a person may be looking at when the person's eyes are closed. Now, they will only turn to look if the person's eyes are open! Before they've even hit their first birthday, infants have learned the eyes are important sources of information they can use to figure out what a person may be looking at and thinking about.

By 12 months, a toddler will not only follow the direction of an adult's gaze, but will move to a place where she can view from the same direction as the adult (for example, peering around a door). She is aware the adult sees something she does not (Tomasello et al., 2005; Meltzoff, 2007). At the same time, she is now ready to share attention to objects with another person. This is the essence of joint attention. The toddler is now able to utilize all she has learned: she can look, talk, and gesture to gain attention *and* direct attention to someone or something of interest.

Why is this important? Babies who were good gaze followers at 10 months have been found to have larger vocabularies and create more complex sentences when they are toddlers (Meltzoff and Brooks, 2009). Thinking about this from a social perspective, we know that infants who are good gaze followers look longer at a target object when an adult is looking in the same direction (Meltzoff et al., 2007). It is as if the object carries special importance because it has the adult's attention. Infants who are able to make this experience-sharing leap have created a situation where a responsive adult is likely to offer a label to map language onto the joint encounter. For example, a baby who follows an adult's line of vision to a passing airplane is likely to hear that adult say, "Yes, that's an *airplane*." Research shows that this bidirectional experience (e.g., the adult sees the child trying to see what an adult sees so the adult then labels the object with language) leads to a language learning advantage, which will follow the infant into her school-aged years (Meltzoff and Brooks, 2009).

Although it emerges somewhat earlier for functional and joint attention purposes (Carpenter, Nagell & Tomasello, 1998), at 12 months toddlers understand **pointing** as a social reference tool, and they are able to use it to get another person to attend to their intention and/or share an experience. Children of this age can point to influence what an adult is thinking (Liebal et al., 2009). They already know they can make an adult look at, pick up, and deliver an object just by pointing at it.

Pointing is unique. Unlike nodding, pretending to drink from a cup, wagging your finger, or holding up a hand to say "stop," it does not have a specific meaning. A point by itself is only a means to direct attention. To *comprehend* the point, the individuals involved must share a context and perspective: we know some things together and we both know that we both know. To infer the social intention of the pointer, participants must rely heavily on the common ground between them (Behne, Carpenter and Tomasello, 2005).

> Before they've even hit their first birthday, infants have learned the eyes are important sources of information they can use to figure out what a person may be looking at and thinking about.

At the same time, adults and children are engaging in triadic interactions such as building a block tower or completing a puzzle together. These activities are more "coordinated joint engagement," since the child can take both roles (e.g., placing the block or holding it steady) and can also help the adult if needed (Tomasello et al., 2005).

By 18 months, toddlers not only have a basic understanding of the desires of others *and* how they might be different from their own, they are able to act on that knowledge in the service of others. Repacholi and Gopnick (1997) proved that toddlers were able to act upon the preferences of others, regardless of their own feelings. How did they do this? They showed two groups of children images of the reactions of a researcher who had tasted broccoli and crackers. One group of children viewed disgusted reactions to broccoli and delighted reaction to crackers. The second group was shown the opposite reactions. Subsequently, the children were asked to share their own food with the researcher. At 15 months, children offered only crackers, a food they preferred. By 18 months, they offered whichever food they had seen the researcher enjoy, *regardless* of their own preferences. Clearly, by 18 months toddlers are able to employ facial expressions and other context clues to read someone else's plan and, then, to use this information to inform their own behavior.

Development of Cooperation

At the same time infants are developing the capacities for collaborative intentions, they are also developing the skills and motivation to *share* them: to **cooperate**. The drive to cooperate, which develops as early as 14–18 months, is a unique form of social engagement. It involves shared goals, shared attention, and a shared plan of action (intention), the ability to read another person's plan (theory of mind) and the intrinsic motivation to help the person accomplish it. If we make a plan to go pick apples from a tree whose branches are higher than either of us can reach, we need to make a joint intention ("we intentionality") and then each play our appropriate roles to make that happen. For example, I can climb the ladder to get us the apples, but that will only happen if you hold the ladder so I don't fall.

> The drive to cooperate, which develops as early as 14–18 months, is a unique form of social engagement.

We know that cooperation is innate because we are not the only primates who engage in this behavior (chimps do, too!) and because rewards do not increase it. In fact, research shows that extrinsic rewards, such as receiving toys as a reward for cooperative acts, decreases a student's innate altruistic desire to cooperate (Tomasello, 2009)!

To test this out, researchers developed a series of experiments designed to show children's altruistic behaviors. The experiment consisted of two parts: a treatment phase where individual children, 20 months of age, were given the opportunity to help the adult and offered a verbal reward (praise), a material reward (chance to play an attractive game) or no reward at all (neutral response). Children who helped in the treatment phase moved on to the test phase. In the test phase, no reward was offered. The hypothesis of the experimenters was that children with intrinsic motivation to help would not be impacted by external rewards. They also hypothesized verbal or social rewards would have no effect or possibly a positive effect on increasing behavior.

Results revealed several things. First and foremost, 20-month-olds are intrinsically motivated to help. Even more interesting, after experiencing praise or a neutral response, children were equally helpful to the examiner as compared to those who received material rewards. Children who received a reward during the initial phase were, in fact, less likely to help. Furthermore, the offer of an extrinsic motivation served to diminish the helping behavior in the long run. This study suggests that children are less inclined to develop a spirit of cooperation or helpfulness when they are offered external rewards. It's as if the reward shifted the focus from the altruistic act to a more narcissistic act (I will only do things when I get an extrinsic reward). This, in turn, suggests that altruism or the desire to help is innate (Warneken and Tomasello, 2008). It also represents a paradigm shift in terms of reinforcement. If the desire to help is innate and external reinforcers do not increase the behavior, then teaching children the *why* beneath the behavior will be far more important than training the skill in a stimulus response manner. This desire to help, which is so closely aligned with cooperation (and our old friend, theory of mind) is intertwined with self-regulation and executive function.

Development of Individual Self-Regulation and Executive Function

As the fundamental skills of social engagement and social monitoring are developing, so too are children learning the self-control, individual self-regulation and executive function skills required to use their observations to make a plan to get what they want or solve a problem. At its highest levels, executive functioning skills allow us to set a goal, take into account our previous experiences to determine the steps to achieve the goal, initiate the steps, evaluate our progress, and know when we have hit the mark. When something goes awry, executive function skills help us assess the damage and modify our approach.

Underlying the capacity for goal setting and goal attainment is self-control and individual self-regulation. The early foundations of trust and self-awareness toddlers gain as a result of secure attachments with caregivers result in them becoming increasingly active and willing to explore their world. As babies, their ability to stay regulated came from adults who cared for them consistently. When they cried, an attentive parent was quick to figure out what was wrong and fix the situation so the baby could regain calm. As toddlers, children learn to wait for what they want and yet they are also more assertive and goal oriented. They see what they want and move to get it. Caregivers, in return, are starting to set limits and have expectations for behavior.

At around two years of age, toddlers, while still very impulse driven, are beginning to develop the ability to set a goal and follow several steps to reach it. Unfortunately, they are not as able to assess their ability to follow those steps and we all know what happens when their outcomes do not meet their plans or when their desires surpasses their ability to express themselves.

Around the same age, children's desire to communicate a feeling outstrips their ability to express it through facial expression and behavior. They have the feeling, they *know* they have the feeling, but they are not yet able to communicate it. To solve this problem, they begin to use emotional words like *mad, happy,* and *scared* (Bloom, 1998). Such word learning is intimately connected to what children are thinking and feeling, demonstrating what is known as the *principle of relevance.* However, a contrasting *principle of discrepancy* also comes into play. "Language has to be learned when what the child has in mind differs from what someone else has in mind and must be expressed to be shared" (Bloom, 1998). To stay connected to others, children must be able to express and understand how they and others feel, when that feeling is the same and especially when it is different.

> The work of a typical three-year-old is all about self-regulation, emotional regulation and learning to exist within the needs of the group.

By the time a child is three years old, the capacity for individual self-regulation and self-control as well as the fundamentals of executive functioning enable them to imagine a goal and then plan and execute the necessary tasks to participate in group activities and learn in a preschool classroom. They build upon their capacity to regulate themselves as individuals to learn how to regulate themselves within a group. They are able to avoid forbidden behaviors to keep their teachers feeling good about them and to subvert their own desires in the service of a group goal, a group experience, or because the needs of another overrides their own.

> Three-year-olds know that people may want, feel or like different things than they do but they are not yet fully aware that they also have different *thoughts.*

The work of a typical three-year-old is all about self-regulation, emotional regulation and learning to exist within the needs of the group. A flexible preschooler knows he needs to wait for assistance with a jacket if the teacher is helping another child tie a shoe, can think about something else or listen attentively even when he is not entirely interested, or can wait for a turn to talk if another child is answering the question or making a comment. All of these skills are those that are present in a child who is able to self-regulate in a group.

Development of Central Coherence and Theory of Mind

Children are well on their way to developing a theory of mind by their third year of life (Leslie, 1994). While babies can understand another person's desires based on observing that person's physical actions, that's a far cry from understanding that others have *different* beliefs. Three-year-olds know that people may want, feel or like different things than they do but they are not yet fully aware that they also have different *thoughts.* We know this through well-established experiments that test "false beliefs." One such test is the famous Wimmer and Perner *Sally-Anne* test (1983). In this, children are told a story involving two characters and two receptacles for objects. One character (Sally) watches the other stow the object, let's say in a closet. The second character (Anne) leaves the room and Sally moves the object from the closet to under the bed. Children are then asked where Anne will look for the object when she returns to the room. They pass if they say the closet and fail if they extrapolate from their own knowledge and say under the bed. To pass the task, children must be able to understand they know something Anne does not and be able to predict what Anne will do based on what Anne knows, not on what they know.

Four-year-olds can pass this test; they can articulate a theory of mind. Although they may not be able to define the concept of thought, we know they understand it. How do we know? They use language that clearly demonstrates they are thinking about what other people are thinking, by using words such as *think, know, guess, decide,* and *forget* to talk about their own or other's mental states. A four-and-a-half-year-old boy was overheard saying to his mother, "Mom, did you remember to close the cage or did you forget again?" When looking at the language of fours and fives in context, we observe that they are talking about, and therefore thinking about, the contents of the mind and not just objects and actions.

How does the concept of *self and others* develop? Through the first 12–14 months, children are driven by biological and social emotional need. Their understanding of self extends only as far as they are compelled to satisfy their physical desires for food, drink, stimulation and sleep as well as their social emotional desires to relate. Between 18 and 24 months, children begin to recognize themselves in the mirror. They become aware that whatever they do, the person in the mirror does the same thing or they begin to rub at a spot of dirt on their own face when they see one on their reflection. Simultaneously, we see a linguistic demonstration of this mental idea: toddlers begin to use the pronouns "me" and "mine." Between the ages of three and four, demonstrations of theory of mind emerge as preschoolers understand that you may know something different from what they know. Finally, by five years old, they have developed a sophisticated understanding: they know some things, you know some things, and, most important, *you know that they know and they know that you know*!

Once children are aware that others have thoughts and they develop the ability to talk about each other's thoughts, they can begin to figure out what *other* people do and do not know. This increase in language-based skills and theory of mind work in tandem to create more sophisticated thinking. Simon Baron-Cohen (2001) in quoting Grice regards this as especially important because it helps people follow one of the most important rules of communication: *don't tell other people something they already know*. Three-year-olds are already aware that if another person can *see* something, they must know about it. They have already made the connection between gaze direction and thinking and gaze direction and knowing. Four-year-olds are able to use this information and what they infer about its context to decide what a conversational or play partner does and does not know and, therefore, what that partner does and does not need to know during that interaction.

This matters because to be a successful play partner, children need to be able to talk about what they are thinking and think about what another person is saying and doing to collaborate and coordinate their plans. Children need to be flexible enough to join their plan to another person's or to allow another person to make the plan. And, children also need to be able to infer meaning from context and know that although a metal strainer is a kitchen implement when it is draining spaghetti, it can also be a space helmet if they are pretending together to take a trip into outer space. If children over-focus on the holes they do not see that the shape of a strainer and perhaps its metal composition lend themselves perfectly to pretending it is a helmet.

This ability to analyze and synthesize relevant information and details of a situation to see how the information fits into the large whole is known in the research as **central coherence**. This ability to "see the big picture" or synthesize information is also a crucial process involved in the formulation of a concept. For example, most young children learn early on that dogs are four-legged creatures. They then go through a period of overgeneralization where most or even all four-legged creatures they see are dogs. Gradually they become aware that there are many animals with four legs and that each has its own unique sound and set of physical features. This ability to classify and compare objects, events and ideas based on individual features and the context in which they emerge is crucial to the understanding and interpretation of social interactions and social behavior.

> To be a successful play partner, children need to be able to talk about what they are thinking and think about what another person is saying and doing. ▪

Development of Collaborative Play

Successfully engaging in cooperative pretend play requires acting out a pretend episode *and* the capacity to make sense of what your play partner is doing. This ability to read the plan of another person begins as early as 24 months. Two great examples of this are the toy horse and dirty pig experiments (Harris, Kavanaugh and Dowson, 1994, 1997). In the first, a researcher pretends to pour water onto one of two plastic horses. A child is given a towel and asked to dry the "wet" horse. The child has to decide which horse to dry. Children below two years of age were inconsistent, drying one or the other by chance. Two-year-olds, however, were largely correct in their choices. They dried the "wet" horse.

In a second, similar experiment, the same researchers pretended to squirt ketchup on a toy pig. Children are then shown three pictures (one plain, one with a white mark on its back, one with a red blob) and asked which one portrays what happened to the pig. The results were very consistent: children under two years of age were erratic in their choices; children over two years consistently picked the pig with the ketchup blob. Even though they saw no water poured and no ketchup squirted, two-year-olds consistently intuited the results of the experimenters' pretend plan.

So now we come to one of the highpoints of preschool social development: cooperative *and* collaborative pretend play. Neurotypical children come to the classroom able to share meaning, read another person's plan, develop a shared plan, and then play a reciprocal role in making it happen. This advanced understanding of the mind, one's own and others', supports the ability to participate in group imaginative cooperative play. Not only are they able to cooperate and play within their own or another person's plan, without the assistance of an adult, they are also able to collaborate with others and make a joint plan, share their imaginations with each other and come up with a joint action schema to be enacted together.

In general children want to play and want to keep their friends engaged in playing with them. This desire to play with others and to *keep* playing with others underlies the developing capacity to self-regulate in a group and be flexible as they take perspective of their own and other's needs. It enables them to accept restrictions on their behavior and rules that they might not necessarily abide by in other situations. Thinking back to our five preschoolers in the housekeeping corner, to continue the play the "baby" has to accept the controls over his behavior ("babies can't talk") and stay silent if he wants to play in this group. The ability to do this, to participate in these collaborative play experiences, has a bidirectional influence on self-control, which is fundamental to social success (Vygotsky, 1966).

Playing as a group requires the ability to communicate your own ideas; it also involves being flexible enough to imagine and accept the ideas of others.

So what are the skills that form the foundation for being a good "player"? Now that preschoolers are able to separate the contents of their mind (thoughts) from the reality of the situation, they are ripe for being able to pretend. Pretending a stick is a horse means you have to keep both ideas separate but always in your mind. Lillard (1998) writes about two levels of pretending with others.

The first involves the *negotiations*: you be the cowboy, I'll be the horse. A great deal of perspective taking is required to carry this out. You also need language to create, explain, maintain and correct the social pretend play experience. For instance, if you are playing the horse and get behind the wheel of a car, your partner is going to remind you, "You can't do that—horses can't drive." This negotiating is incredibly important. The success of the play scheme and making sure that no one deviates from the scenario or leaves the game, rests on meshing of ideas, compromising on the rules, reading other people's plans and emotional reactions, and repairing when mistakes in interpretation occur. If not, people leave and then the game is over, perhaps before it has even begun.

The second level of pretending is the actual *playing*. Remembering that pretend play requires a mental representation (a thought) means that you have to keep in mind the plan. If a broom is a horse, you must remember to think about it that way. How do horses move, communicate, and interact? Engaging in advanced role-play, which involves taking on the role of a different type of person (e.g., cowboy, chef, etc.) and acting like another person or thing, requires thinking about that person and having an understanding of their thoughts, beliefs, feelings, and desires to know how *that person* would behave.

Playing as a group requires the ability to communicate your own ideas; it also involves being flexible enough to imagine and accept the ideas of others (Segal, 2004). Children go through very clear and distinct stages as they move from solitary pretend play (19–22 months) to parallel play (I am aware you are doing things and I am doing things but we are not interacting), through associative play to full cooperative play. Associative play (24–36 months) is when a group of toddlers may all be doing the same thing, sharing materials or hanging out in the same pretend play corner. However there is no planning, nor dialogue, about who will do what and who will play which role.

Neurotypical learners at age four are able to share in the imagination of others, not just their own. They can collaborate on play schemes, adding and building upon the ideas of others, and meshing them with their own to come up with a new scheme. They can flexibly incorporate others' thoughts and imagination into their own play scheme to allow a new collaborative play idea to emerge. Although it has a distinct social purpose, collaborative play skills are also *critical* for the development of crucial later skills involved in working as part of a classroom group, participating in conversation, solving personal problems, developing meaningful relationships, imagining a goal and seeing it through and comprehending character and plot developments in text. Collaborative or social pretend play is significant as the platform for socialization and the acquisition of social knowledge. While collaborating on play scripts, children mutually explore social roles and issues of intimacy, trust, negotiation, and the ability to compromise. To do this, children must also master the communication skills required to convey their ideas and consider the ideas of others. In preschool and early learning we call this collaborative play. As children get older we call it having a discussion or working together as a team.

Why does play matter so much? Vygotsky (1966) talks about the idea that play is a child's imagination enacted and later, when one reaches adolescence, imagination is play without action. Being a good player at three, four and five has a direct connection to dreaming a dream, imagining a life and seeing it through. Play is to young children as conversation is to adolescents and adults.

Learning in a Group of 20–30 Children

These same skills of abstract thinking, collaboration and communication underlie the child's growing awareness and appreciation of the perspectives of others, a capacity we know is critical for socialized thought and the developmental milestone necessary for learning in a larger group as well as the growth of friendship and intimate relationships.

> Children who are educated in play-based environments have the added advantage of being strong problem solvers, more flexible thinkers, and better at collaboration. ■

The Common Core State Standards, adopted to date by 45 of the 50 U.S. states and three of its territories, include a section on conversation under the title, *Speaking and Listening*. Kindergarten students are expected to "participate in collaborative conversations with diverse partners about kindergarten topics and texts with peers and adults in small and large groups." And, to "follow agreed upon rules for discussions (e.g., listening to others and taking turns speaking about the topics and texts under discussion) and continue a conversation through multiple exchanges, ask and answer questions in order to seek help, get information or clarify something that is not understood." (Common Core State Standards Initiative, 2010) The social operating system required to meet these goals is assumed in the preschool and early elementary aged child. It is presumed that as a member of a pre-academic learning classroom children are good to go and their social capacities are functioning. It is not expected that children will need to be taught these skills when they reach preschool or kindergarten.

Knowing this, it is counterintuitive to be spending precious time teaching academic skills in preschool. Unfortunately, the trend toward early academics in the preschool classroom is overlooking the fact that the *work* of early childhood is *play*. School programs that are overly focused on letters, numbers, and pre-academics are taking critical time away from pretend play and socialization. These key elements of child development and crucial foundational capacities which underlie the ability to learn in a group and engage in sophisticated conversation at age level expectation are not given enough focus when too much time is spent learning letter and number facts.

The No Child Left Behind Act of 2001 and other results-oriented educational legislation and regulation have led to a preschool and kindergarten curricula more focused on this "academic" approach. In early 2002, the National Reporting System (NRS) instituted required standardized testing in Head Start twice per year, to assess language, pre-literacy, and pre-math skills. As opponents of this predicted, the U.S. Government Accountability Office found in 2005 that at least 18% of Head Start programs had changed their instruction to meet the content of the NRS testing.

Why is this a problem? Longitudinal research (Miller and Almon, 2009) on curriculum design has proven that early teaching of phonics and other discrete reading skills does not lead to long-term academic gains. In fact, the opposite is true; engagement in pretend play has been found to be significantly (and positively) correlated with text comprehension, meta-linguistic awareness, and understanding of the purpose of reading and writing. Moreover, children who are educated in play-based environments have the added advantage of being strong problem solvers, more flexible thinkers, and better at collaboration—important traits that define a successful adult (Miller and Almon, 2009).

What happens when children don't develop play or have difficulty playing with others or when they don't have the ability to self-regulate in a group? The literature on peer election (picking friends) and peer rejection tells us that a delay in reading others' plans, which will lead to difficulty with collaborative pretend play, will have a significant impact on the development of peer relations (Slaughter, Dennis and Pritchard, 2002). Children who are good at playing are more likely to be chosen as playmates and will spend more time experiencing and practicing social interactions that ultimately facilitate their ability to read other people's plans. Simply said, if I am a good player, more people want to play with me. The more I engage with others, the more I learn about how to consider my own and others' minds simultaneously, as we work to resolve issues and imagine new situations in which we can cooperate. This means I get to practice being a good player and resolving conflicts when I am not so good a player and I will get better and better at it with practice. Actively engaging the social mind is self-perpetuating and is at the root of the development of many socially related concepts and skills required of us as we get older (written expression, reading comprehension of fiction, playground play, working as part of a group in a classroom, participating in a meeting, building a social network, holding a job, getting married, having one's own family, etc.).

A national study (Gilliam, 2005) discovered that nearly 7 of 1000 children across the country were being expelled from regular education preschools, most of them because of difficulty self-regulating in a group, reading and following the plan of others, and/or sharing an imagination. From our clinical experience, there are many more students who come into kindergarten with academic prowess, yet struggle in the classroom environment. Their challenges with spontaneous peer play (and the attendant skill set one learns as a result of positive peer play) have a significant impact on their ability to learn to work as part of a classroom group. (See page 16, Major Milestones of Social Development.)

We need to reorient our thinking, and shift the paradigm to incorporate social thinking instruction in regular education classes. Social learning is a national issue; it is NOT only a special education issue. Many children, not just those with a diagnosis, are arriving at preschool without the requisite skills, social knowledge and self-regulatory control to exist in the classroom and learn in a group. Now, more than ever before, teaching Social Thinking must become an integral part of ALL preschool and early elementary curricula.

When Social Development Goes Awry: What is a Social Learning Challenge?

Let's return to our friends in the housekeeping corner in the preschool classroom. Five four-year-olds—Thomas, Esther, Alison, Angel and Enrique – are still playing in a group. We pick up just after Thomas has told Angel babies can't talk and therefore, he has to be quiet. Angel, who was already upset at having to pretend to be a baby (after all, he is clearly not a baby) looks up from his "crib" and begins to scream and bang his fists on the floor, "Yes I can, yes I can, yes I can." Confused by the outburst, Thomas attempts to pacify Angel and explains babies don't talk until they are older, but that he can say "mama or dada" if he wants. "I can talk, I'm not a baby, I can talk, I'm not a baby, I can talk," continues Angel, louder and louder until the other children start to move away and a teacher intervenes.

● ● ●

Major Milestones of Social Development

Pictured here we see highlights of the ages and stages of the important underpinnings of solid social ability from birth to five years of age.

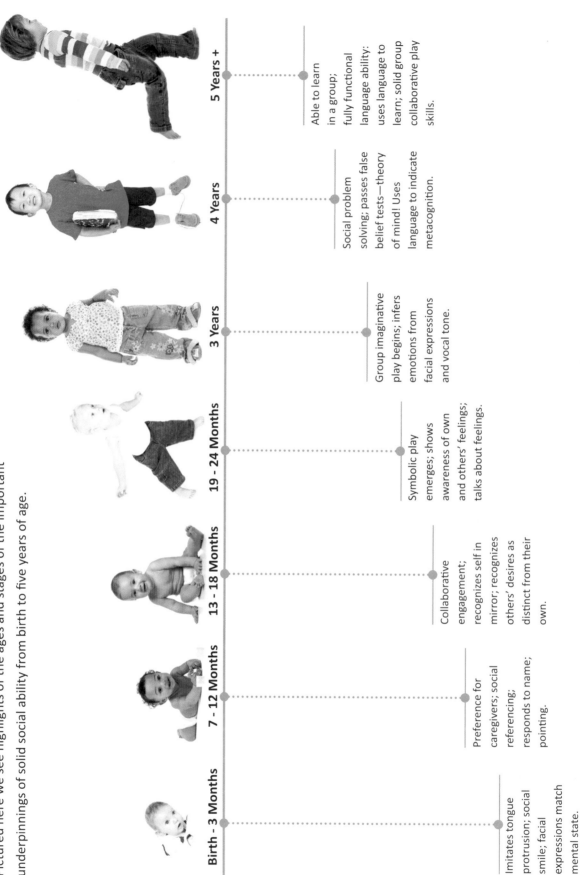

Birth - 3 Months

Imitates tongue protrusion; social smile; facial expressions match mental state.

7 - 12 Months

Preference for caregivers; social referencing; responds to name; pointing.

13 - 18 Months

Collaborative engagement; recognizes self in mirror; recognizes others' desires as distinct from their own.

19 - 24 Months

Symbolic play emerges; shows awareness of own and others' feelings; talks about feelings.

3 Years

Group imaginative play begins; infers emotions from facial expressions and vocal tone.

4 Years

Social problem solving; passes false belief tests—theory of mind! Uses language to indicate metacognition.

5 Years +

Able to learn in a group; fully functional language ability: uses language to learn; solid group collaborative play skills.

Alice's parents are so proud of her language and her ability to remember so many things she sees and hears. They could not believe after only one week of preschool she could recite the names of every child in her class. Not only that, when asked over dinner what she did at school, she was able to tell them every activity from the start of the day to the end by name and also by time. "At 8:30 we had circle, at 9:00 it was choice time, at 9:45 we had a snack," and so on. Imagine their surprise when they were asked in October to come in and discuss a few concerning episodes at school. The teachers began by confirming Alice's large vocabulary and memory for dates and times. However, unlike her parents, they did not necessarily see these as an asset. In fact, they were concerned about her tendency to recite lists and her over-focus on time and reported that these behaviors were interfering with her relationships in the classroom. The teachers offered an anecdote about circle time. The group was headed to the rug area and Alice noted a child was already seated in her favorite spot. Without a thought, Alice pushed the child aside and proceeded to sit on the pink flowers (pink being a favorite color). When the other child began to cry, Alice was seemingly unaware and was truly shocked when she was asked to give up her spot and leave the circle. This led to a tantrum that lasted quite a while, until Alice fell asleep in exhaustion. When she awakened and attempts were made to exact an apology, it became apparent to her teachers that not only was Alice completely unaware of what she had done that might be upsetting, she did not know the other child's name after six weeks in the same classroom. "But," protested her parents, "she knows all the children's names, ask her, she will tell you." "Yes," replied her teachers, "she can recite a list of their names, but she cannot match the names to any of the children, even to Abby who shares her cubby."

● ● ●

Joseph loved walking to preschool with his mother. Every day they saw the dog next door digging holes in the lawn, the post woman delivering mail in her very small car, the new house going up right before their eyes and the crossing guard on the corner who said, "Hello little man," as they crossed in front of the playground. It was one of his favorite times of day and if the credits began to roll on the morning news and they were not putting on their coats, Joseph would begin to get agitated. One day, his mother was ill and his father stayed home later to take Joseph to school. As always, Joseph was ready and waiting by the door just as the final credits ended. His father emerged from the kitchen with his car keys and started toward the garage door, "Come on Joseph, time to go." Joseph fell to the ground in a heap and began to cry. "But we don't drive to preschool, we walk."

● ● ●

Jayden loves attending preschool and talks with his mother about the other children, the toys, the guinea pigs and the other exciting things he sees and hears. He runs excitedly up the stairs each morning, tracing the lines on the staircase and the edge of the cinderblocks on the wall leading to his cubby. At circle time, he sits on the periphery tracing the shapes on the rug, often missing the cue to stand up and put his picture on the attendance chart. His teachers begin to notice how every object and toy becomes part of his train fascination. Initially they are impressed with his creativity, but slowly they begin to realize Jayden never chooses to engage in cooperative play with others, unless of course they are willing to make a train out of the blocks. On the playground, Jayden has a hard time joining in. Most days he can be found watching the others play and tracing his finger along the many lines and shapes he finds on the fence, the jungle gym and the slide.

● ● ●

Lauren and Jose are in the dress up corner. Jose immediately reaches for the stethoscope and tongue depressor and says, "I'll be the doctor and you be the patient." Play commences and Lauren arrives at the doctor's office with a sore throat and a headache. Jose completes his examination, prescribes medicine and bed-rest and sends Lauren on her way. Lauren "walks" out the waiting room "door" and then turns around and says, "Ok, now I'll be the doctor and you be the patient." "Oh no," says Jose, "I said I'll be the doctor, NOT you." A short argument ensues during which Jose stands his ground. After a few minutes, Lauren walks away in frustration leaving Jose alone. Jose is genuinely confused and goes to report to the teacher Lauren left in the middle of their game.

> Most kids are born with a brain that helps them intuitively learn to observe social information around them, their "social radar."

Most kids are born with a brain that helps them to "think with their eyes," to intuitively learn to observe social information in the world around them, ultimately helping them to observe how people think and feel about each other. This "social radar" (Winner, 2000, 2007) also helps them observe interpersonal interactions and intuit the hidden rules in each context. For example, nobody tells children how close or how far away to stand to someone else while waiting for a turn on the slide or that it is okay to teasingly call another child a poopy-head when you are being silly together on the playground, but not when that person is not your friend and it is certainly not okay to say that to your teacher or grandmother. Social radar also helps them understand they can pretend to be something they aren't and utilize what they know to make the pretense "real."

Some kids do not have this social radar and some kids have it but are just not tuned in to the right channel. They just don't see how and why using their eyes to read the situation will help them accurately interpret other people's reactions to their behavior and they don't understand why reading someone else's plan makes playing together so much more fun.

For some children, although they have the fundamental tools of language their communication ability does not support them in ways that facilitate their play-based interactions or help them engage in basic expected social experiences with classmates. Some of these same children may be considered advanced in their language development and may have even started to learn to decode text (read) all on their own. Still other children may not have developed the tools they need to adapt to changing contexts and reciprocal play or conversation-based interactions or they just can't figure out what the problem is, much less what needs to be done. Or, they simply don't know how to join or stay with the group.

Many kids can play and imagine about their own thoughts, but have not yet figured out how to share in the imagination of others. They never quite followed the pathway from parallel play to associative play, and this is often where our kids are falling apart. They are watching other kids but are not using other kids as models or mentors for their own play. They don't engage in imitative play or when watching someone else do something they think looks interesting say to themselves, "Oooo that's a good idea, I'm going to try that."

Still others may have figured out how to share play with others, but only when an adult is running the show because they are used to taking direction from the adult (who is actively engaged in social problem solving) about what to do with their peers. However, when it comes to spontaneous peer-directed collaborative play, they are neither able to take direction from peers nor share an imagination with them. Somewhere between the ages of two and three they are falling behind because they are not imitating others, pretending together and learning to collaborate for a shared purpose. Some of these children will eventually be diagnosed with social cognitive difficulty. Still others may not have had the early experiences they need due to decreased opportunity, overuse of technological media, and other environmental factors.

There are some children who have difficulty with sensory processing, who have neurological thresholds that are outside the norm of expectations and whose nervous systems do not respond in typical ways. They may also have difficulty accessing the necessary self-regulation strategies to help them manage sensory input as it comes their way. Handling the many challenges that arise due to sensory issues is beyond the scope of this current early learning curriculum. We refer you to *The Zones of Regulation®* (Kuypers, 2011) and The SCERTS® Model (Prizant, Wetherby, Rubin, Laurent & Rydell, 2007) for more information on this.

To date, most of the research about young children with social cognitive learning challenges involves the *significantly* challenged learners, NOT the children who have acquired language but are talking in a pedantic way. These students, with their strong vocabularies but who are not relational to their peers, have not been well documented. The attention of researchers has been on the more obviously delayed children, those who are so far off the developmental charts that they are not yet candidates for learning through language or a cognitive behavioral approach.

Why is this even an issue? Despite what may appear at first glance to be elevated functioning, the children we are referring to struggle nonetheless and their need for concrete social teaching often goes unchecked. They may have huge vocabularies but what good is that if they can't use their words to connect with their peers during conversation or to engage in joint interactive play? As infants they may have developed the basic reciprocity, language and even imitation skills with adults who helped them along the way. However, when symbolic play skills emerged, they became stuck in solitary and parallel play. They never moved on to more abstract symbolic, associative and cooperative play where they are able to share an imagination with another, co-create a play scheme and engage in the necessary collaboration and cooperation to make it happen. Language may be strong in these kids but we shouldn't be teased into assuming more; their social thinking may be decidedly lacking.

> Language may be strong in these "higher functioning" kids but we shouldn't be teased into assuming more; their social thinking may still be decidedly lacking.

Beyond language, the profile of these kids reveals more strengths and equally profound weaknesses. They may have singular knowledge that goes deep and broad into areas not typically found in preschool curriculum. Yet they are unable to share this knowledge with others in a way that engages them and helps others share in the enthusiasm. They are great "talkers" and may be good decoders but may still struggle with comprehending what they read. They can be good singular players, able to busy themselves contentedly but are not truly relational when it comes to developing connections with others near the level of their age-mates. Often parents report these children achieved many developmental academic milestones on time, or even early. Their parents have celebrated these islands of knowledge and through these celebrations and the efforts made to reinforce their "genius" have quietly given them permission not to play with peers and not to engage. Even those kids who have an established core set of skills, it is likely they cannot use them flexibly and across settings.

The social radar these children lack can result in them missing the social cues that neurotypical kids process easily. So, they are unaware that Grandma, who loves them to death, will listen to them talk about iguanas from morning until night, but a peer is at some point going to get bored and walk away or tell them to stop. They are not reading the cues of the peer listener, the shifting from foot to foot, the occasional glances in the direction of a group who really seem to be having a lot of fun or worse, they keep talking and talking as the peer is turning around and walking away. They may not even realize that reading these cues is part of our expected social functioning!

So many of our children are so focused on their thoughts, or are so focused on the details that interest them, that they are not getting or learning from the big picture. They are not taking into account the context of the situation (central coherence) and making smart guesses about what a person is thinking or feeling based on their gaze direction, facial expression or behavior. Often they get stuck on a detail (and perhaps the wrong detail) and miss the all-important message. For instance, putting up one finger to indicate something (the detail) means one thing when you are counting (context), another when you are pointing at an interesting action going on around you (context) and yet another when you are trying to tell someone what you want (context). If the child misses the social intention of the finger gesture and instead focuses on an interesting ring, bracelet, glove or mark on the hand, that child is pretty much lost in interpreting the behavior.

> Context is so important. When we know the context, we can make predictions about what will happen and what is expected of us.

Neurotypical children are able to note that detail and consider it within the context to help them form an assumption about the behavior. They are also able to filter this detail through their own experiences and make a smart guess about the other person's intention. For instance, if Gabriella puts up her finger to indicate how many pieces of apple she wants and says "one," it's clear what she means. If Gabriella is pointing and looking back she might want me to look at something and if she is pointing at an orange rather than the apple she is using that same gesture to make a choice instead. Children with social cognitive challenges will sometimes miss the context and therefore have a hard time figuring out the other person's intention.

Context is so important. Danish psychologist Peter Vermeulen, author of the intriguing book, *Autism as Context Blindness*, puts forth his theory that at the heart of the autism spectrum, children struggle because of their inability to accurately perceive and respond to the contexts of their environments. When we know the context, we can make predictions about what will happen and what is expected of us. Context helps us focus our attention on what is important and it is context that helps us problem solve situations that are not entirely clear. Knowing about the context of birthday parties means we can think about what we remember from other such events and predict there will be music (hopefully not too loud), presents (not for us but for the birthday child), cake (with any luck a flavor we like), treats and games (maybe I'll win and get a prize). For the child who has a hard time recognizing context, mentioning an upcoming birthday party does not automatically arouse those

Diagram 2: The Shaky Foundation When Social Development Goes Awry
Here we see that if the fundamental capacities are not fully developed or if there are gaps in certain areas, the foundation is weak and our student does not have all the tools to join and play at the level of his or her peers.

kinds of thoughts. So when Will arrives at the party and it's loud and chaotic, he will probably be unprepared for the experience and become agitated or upset. Sometimes these children just don't have the underlying executive functions that allows them to develop event-related schema to compare one experience with another to recognize what's the same (predictable) and what's different. Imagine how chaotic the world must be to the child for whom every situation seems new and/or strange and he is not able to recognize similar situations and therefore guess or know what will happen next.

Diagram 2 illustrates what can happen when children don't have the solid foundation of social developmental skills that foster later social success. The impairments may fall on a continuum from mild to severe, but the outcome will generally be the same if unchecked and unattended: there will be lasting challenges with social learning that will impact all areas of functioning.

Why Teach Social Thinking in Preschool and Early Elementary?

For children who are melting down because they don't understand what is happening around them, for children who are so singular minded and unable to learn and play in a group that they are being asked to leave their preschool daily, weekly or worse, permanently, for kids who struggle to learn as part of a group in their early elementary school classrooms, finding a way to reach and teach these children about their social functioning is paramount.

Social Thinking is a cognitive behavioral approach that teaches complex social concepts in a concrete yet appealing manner. Michelle Garcia Winner, who founded the Social Thinking framework over two decades ago, recognized that another way was needed to teach language-based learners (young and old) about their social selves and their social brains. She discovered that these students benefitted from being taught the *why of* social decision making. Merely teaching rote social skills (the *what*) was not enough for these verbal learners. Furthermore, this approach helped them learn to generalize their social learning across settings. Therefore, the intervention is aimed at teaching the thought process that underlies the social behavior, which increases children's ability to flexibly think and shift behavior to the demands of the situation.

By incorporating explicit language-based concepts, Winner encouraged children to learn about and practice the core social processing abilities their development seemed to skip over. Through this explicit teaching, students have learned to connect thoughts, feelings and behavior, to recognize the purpose of specific behaviors (social skills), and gain the observational ability to explore social expectations across all settings (context).

The Incredible Flexible You curriculum is designed to help young learners develop the tools they need to be flexible social thinkers. How do we help strengthen their weak foundations? We do this by encouraging the development of social knowledge and self-monitoring of social behaviors by teaching Winner's Social Thinking Vocabulary© and concepts, adapted to the age and social developmental levels of our preschool and early elementary aged students. [1]

---

1 If you are not familiar with the Social Thinking framework or the larger Social Thinking Vocabulary, we recommend Michelle's seminal book, *Thinking About YOU Thinking About ME,* second edition. In that book you will find many more concepts relevant to older and more mature thinkers as well as a wealth of foundational information. Available at www.socialthinking.com.

Previously, we did not have a common vocabulary for talking about complex social concepts and expectations in a concrete way. Instead, we simply expected children to understand intuitively and perceive what is socially appropriate. When they did not, we offered general feedback such as "you need to…," "pay attention," "cooperate" and "be friendly"—never stopping to question whether or not a child who could use those words understood what any of these social concepts really meant.

We have all witnessed these scenarios as they play out in every day situations and the obvious confusion our students with social challenges display. How many students have you met who have been upset because they did not get to play "their way" and tearfully announce that the other students were not friendly or not cooperating, when in fact the student was the one who was failing to cooperate or be friendly? Remembering that the work of our early learners is all about self-regulation, emotional regulation and learning to exist within a group, we can start to appreciate that the metacognitive basis of Social Thinking provides the glue that binds the social foundations together.

> The core concepts of Social Thinking are foundational to all social interactions, regardless of age.

In this curriculum, we have specifically created lessons to teach 10 of the core Social Thinking concepts and vocabulary to our young learners with average to above average language ability and cognition. Social concepts are taught concretely, by making the "understood" explicit. It is not enough to learn to sit quietly and wait when the teacher is talking to someone else. Children need to understand *why* they are sitting quietly and why if they do, they will be rewarded with a teacher's positive attention. In essence, we are trying to help children make the connection between thoughts, feelings and attendant behavior. Doing what is expected gives others good thoughts about us which leads them to have good feelings about us, which in turn causes them to act positively toward us. As a result, we feel good too!

But, can preschool and early elementary school-aged students learn about the social learning process metacognitively (thinking about one's thinking) and through using language to better understand social expectations? The answer is yes. In a 2003 study Choi and Kim reported on a cognitive social learning approach utilized with prekindergarten students who had experienced low peer acceptance. Their findings supported what we have found to be true: focusing on the cognitive learning (utilizing concrete concepts and terminology) increases social know-how and subsequently peer acceptance—because cognitive learning leads to behavioral changes.

A research study by Crooke, Hendrix and Rachman published in the *Journal of Autism and Developmental Disorders* in 2008 demonstrated that by teaching elementary school-aged students Social Thinking Vocabulary, their increased social awareness lead them to shift their social behavior and generalize basic concepts across settings without a direct social skills behavioral intervention.

Today, many classrooms and elementary schools across the United States have adopted this basic vocabulary to facilitate social cooperation and problem solving for all students. Teachers and parents report ease in learning the vocabulary concepts, which in turn makes it simple to use them during the many "teachable moments" (e.g., social conflict) that are part of the daily classroom and home environments.

As the research directs us to recognize that social thinking and social learning is a complex, synergistic process, then teaching at the level of one social behavioral skill at a time is counterintuitive. There are hundreds of hidden rules in any situation and the rules change with age and context. There could never be enough hours in the day to teach all the skills a child would need to be a successful young learner, much less have the social smarts to function as a successful adolescent and adult. This is another reason we need to teach the thinking behind the skills, to promote generalization and our children being able to use a social thinking concept across settings. As the research has demonstrated, teaching social thinking from a cognitive point of view allows us to highlight concepts, which can then be integrated into real-life situations (Crooke et al., 2008).

Our social learning never stops; it is an ongoing process as our children grow and develop in age and maturity. Social know-how becomes more nuanced and complicated with age as relevant information and social expectations shift. Good social thinking has to evolve also, requiring a more sophisticated processing system as well as more advanced ways to respond to keep others feeling good about our interaction. The students who learn Social Thinking Vocabulary concepts early in their structured learning can use this information across their years of school and into adulthood. The core concepts are foundational to all social interactions, regardless of age. Social Thinking becomes the supportive framework that gives students the concepts, language, and social learning experiences they need to optimize their development. (See Diagram 3.)

In this two-volume series, we are taking core Social Thinking lessons and adapting them to address the basic information we expect preschoolers and early elementary learners to be actively acquiring, information that will prepare them to extend and deepen their social learning as they grow up. By doing so, we give children with, and without, social learning challenges the know-how, strategies and practice they need to strengthen their shaky foundations and begin to fill in gaps in social development. The result is students who can learn in a group, share an imagination and become the best social thinkers they can be.

Social Thinking Vocabulary for the Preschool and Early Elementary Years

In this curriculum, ten of the basic Social Thinking Vocabulary concepts are introduced at the preschool and early elementary level. It is important that educators and parents are aware of how they can incorporate this language during teachable moments across the school, home and community day. If children do not have the opportunity to think about and use a word or concept after initial instruction, it is unlikely to become part of their repertoire.

Vocabulary programs that are most effective have several key features:
- They offer many opportunities and avenues for word learning.
- Words are chosen for their utility.
- Teaching is explicit.
- There are multiple opportunities for generalization across contexts. In fact, it is expected that once the vocabulary is introduced it is then used by all caregivers who relate to the child to facilitate their discovery of social learning outside the classroom.

Diagram 3: Social Thinking as a Supportive Framework
Social Thinking is the connection that pulls all of these blocks together for children with social cognitive weaknesses.

Research also tells us the best vocabulary programs teach words in context first through story reading, with multiple exposures to the same text (Beck, Perfetti & McKeown, 1982). They have directed discussions on word meaning and then relate the word back to the context. Subsequently, students are given many exposures to the words across contexts, both at home and school (Beck, Perfetti & McKeown, 1982).

With this in mind we designed *The Incredible Flexible You* curriculum to reflect this format. It is filled with structured activities to help introduce the concepts, but the real teaching comes later as students explore how the concepts they learned in class are relevant everywhere. For example, when we teach students to "think with their eyes," we then continue to point out ways throughout the day that they can observe other people to figure out their plan. For example, when children see their moms standing by the door, shoes on and holding a purse and keys, they can think with their eyes and make a smart guess that it's time to go!

> Unlike teaching a specific social skill, we are not expecting learning for mastery when teaching Social Thinking.

Before delving into the vocabulary concepts, a few more important thoughts are warranted.

1. Although the vocabulary is designed to be taught in a specific order and we believe the concepts build upon each other, once you become familiar with the 10 lessons, it is very important to be flexible—seize the moment! If Lucy arrives in your office crying hysterically because someone used her favorite crayons without asking first, it might be just the right time to introduce the Social Thinking concept *size of the problem* into the discussion. You can (and should) expose the students to the vocabulary and terms before they have a full handle on the concept if the moment is right. In fact, using the vocabulary in context before actually teaching it can often make the learning easier and ultimately deeper.

2. Unlike teaching a specific social skill, we are not expecting learning for mastery when teaching Social Thinking. Social learning is something we all do over our lifespan and as we grow our thinking shifts, changes, and evolves. We are not expecting our students to "master" all of these ideas and behaviors across this one set of lessons; the learning will continue indefinitely. Although we teach the concepts in a linear manner, we want you to remember: we are building synergy. We introduce each new concept and then show how it is married to the others.

    This steps outside the traditional view of teaching social skills. We are trying to create synergistic thinking, to demonstrate how the concepts go together, which is how the neurotypical brain learns social information intuitively. We are, in essence, helping our kids see how we keep all the balls (different social thinking concepts) in the air. At the cognitive behavioral level we have to teach Social Thinking in a linear manner, using a cognitive-linguistic approach. But equally important is helping kids see how and why each of these lessons works collaboratively, one building upon the other, with the goal of creating cooperative play and the ability to learn in a group.

3. Be aware that our students with social learning challenges are much slower to learn these concepts; it takes a *lot* of practice. Don't assume because your student has a good vocabulary that she can easily acquire social

information or quickly understand Social Thinking concepts. Do not expect that by using this curriculum your students will "catch up" to their same-aged peers in social awareness. The curriculum will help them establish base skills. While your students are getting there, the peer group will still move right along further in their own social development. There is no end to social learning for any of us and those who are born to social learning challenges will find this to be something they have to pay extra attention to throughout their lives. As they grow and mature, so will these concepts expand to their thinking level and continue to be taught.

To follow are the 10 Social Thinking Vocabulary concepts spotlighted in the 10 storybooks and lessons that make up *The Incredible Flexible You* curriculum, Volumes 1 and 2. Each volume contains five storybooks and lessons.

1 *Thinking Thoughts and Feeling Feelings*

At the core of social learning is our thoughts and feelings. The ability to engage in perspective taking, play collaboratively and establish friendships with others stems from thoughts: knowing our own, sharing them with others and taking others' thoughts into account as we act and react. We introduce this social concept first because all subsequent concepts and vocabulary lessons are tied back to thoughts. (What are you thinking? What am I thinking? What is the group thinking about?)

We make the connection to feelings because what we think and what we feel are inextricably linked. Thoughts and feelings are abstract concepts and making them comprehensible to young children means offering a small piece of a much bigger whole. Like many concepts children learn in preschool, we introduce them more concretely and as children's understanding grows, we layer on learning until they are able to understand concepts and ideas in more nuanced and abstract ways.

In exploring thoughts and feelings, we begin by establishing a connection to body parts. Preschoolers are familiar with this concept and we are able to use what they know, that we all have many body parts and each part has a job to do. In most cases, we can see these parts and watch them do their jobs. For example, we can see hands clap, hold, and touch and feet tap, jump and run. We then connect that information to the more abstract concepts needed to learn social understanding. That is, there are other body parts, inside our bodies, that have important jobs too. Our brain and heart are two of those parts we use when we are around people. Your brain is your thought maker. We define a thought as an idea, picture, or silent words you have in your brain. To help us talk about thoughts we use words like *think* and *know*. Your heart is your feelings keeper. A feeling is something you feel in your body. To help us talk about our feelings we use words like *happy, sad, mad,* and *scared.*

At this stage we want to raise our students' awareness that they are having thoughts which, in turn, will help them eventually understand that others have thoughts. This is the early stage of teaching perspective taking. We do this by drawing their attention in the beginning to our internal thinking process. For example, if the teacher stands on the table in the classroom we want to label the process and teach the child, "You are having a thought about what the teacher is doing."

Lesson 1 and the related story book introduce the very important concept that we think thoughts and that our thoughts are intimately connected to feelings. It is our expectation that your classroom curricula have already spent a great deal of time exposing children to the basics of feelings, what they are and when they occur. This curriculum is focused on making the connection between thoughts and feelings, a complex social concept, and one we will return to throughout the books and lessons.

In creating this curriculum and trying to define a thought at the most basic level, we took an informal poll of children around the country. Some of their responses follow. We were surprised by some of the eloquent definitions we heard!

"What is a thought?"

- "It's the same thing as ideas and you can think with your brain. You can think about sports and games." Nathan, 4
- "I never met one." Kaleb, 4
- "Something that you think in your head." Sam, 4
- "An idea or imagination." Londyn, 4
- "Something you have to raise your hand for." Noah, 4
- "A thought is quiet." Ben, 4
- "Thinking of something in your brain." Justine, 3.11
- "It's thinking." Alicia, 3
- "When you remember something from before or something that is going to happen." Rylee, 4

"What is thinking?"

- "Something where the brain does the job." Samy, 5
- "A thought you have in your brain." Evan, 5
- "It means you are thinking of something like you are thinking of a star in your dreams." Chakirka, 5
- "Silly, it's when you use your brain!" Rylee, 4
- "Something in your brain...all kinds of stuff and then it comes out of your mouth." Beyonce, 4.2
- "Something you're thinking about. I have a thought in my thinking spot." (When asked where her thinking spot was, she pointed to her heart! Her mom then said, "Oh, I keep my thoughts up in my brain," and Addy said, "Oh yeah, me too!") Addy, 4.1

 *The Group Plan*

To help children learn we are acting as a group, we use the term, "the group plan." This enables them to engage in the thought process that will connect to what they are expected to do. Talking about the group plan helps them focus on, think about, and anticipate the session or class agenda.

We frequently refer to the activities, books and games we are all sharing as "the plan." When children know the plan, they can think about what is expected. This includes the hidden rules and social expectations of the situation, and ultimately helps children think about how we can keep people having good thoughts about us. If the teacher says the plan is to go to circle and read a book, most children know the rule is to find *their* square and sit on it. Yet, how often have we seen the child who is running circles around the beanbag chair when everyone else is listening to the book? If we had asked him, "What's your plan?" we may have discovered that he thought the plan was to imitate the actions of the kids in the book. When we let him in on the fact that the group plan is to *sit* on the beanbag and listen to the story, we give him the social knowledge to change his plan and sit down to join the group. Sometimes, children who are not following the rules simply aren't aware of what the group plan is. As children move into the elementary years, this concept will be enlarged to include reading someone else's plan and understanding their perspective. At the preschool level, the group plan is about following the plan of the group rather than one's own plan, even if it is just a group of two!

3 *Thinking With Your Eyes*

Joint attention, joint intention and acts of emotional engagement are the building blocks that support the social concept we call "thinking with our eyes." Once children understand that other people have thoughts, we teach them that they can use their eyes to figure out what those thoughts might be. We use our eyes to gather information about what other people are looking at and thinking about, what is happening around us and to figure out the group plan. Once children know they need to follow the plan, they learn that thinking with their eyes will give them important information they need to be able to do that.

We "think" with our eyes rather than "look" with our eyes to reinforce the connection to social thinking. Many of our students may look at things and people in their environment, but don't carry the process further to consider the social implications of what they see.

We also use our eyes expressively to let others in on what we are thinking about and to let them know that we are thinking about them when in their presence. When we are sharing an experience, we look at others to let them know we are thinking about *them*, listening to *them*, and talking to *them*.

Thinking with your eyes is a pivotal social thinking concept that can directly influence how well children process and integrate many other of the Social Thinking Vocabulary concepts. And it's anything but "simple" so we caution you not to make assumptions about what your kids with social learning challenges understand from the get go. Teachers and parents should probe a child's level of social ability with regard to this concept. Even many of our verbal and bright early learners may not be able to track the eye gaze of others to know what they are looking at (step 1), or understand that what someone is looking at reflects what that person may be thinking about (step 2).

4 Body in the Group

Once children are able to imitate, engage in joint attention and focused social interaction, they are ready to learn about sharing space effectively. "Body in the group" is the way we talk with our early learners about maintaining a comfortable physical presence around others—not too close, yet not too far. When one's body is in the group, it sends the nonverbal message that you are interested in others and that you are following the same plan. The opposite is also true. If one's body is out of the group (too far away), it sends the message you are not thinking about the group and potentially not interested in being part of it.

5 Whole Body Listening

Students who have a firm foundation of focused attention and the intention to cooperate are ready to learn about "whole body listening." Listening involves more than just hearing words that are being spoken. It includes letting the speaker know we are attentive and engaged. Truesdale (1990) introduced the idea that we use the whole body (eyes, ears, mouths, hands, arms, legs, and feet) when we focus on the group to listen and also to show others that we are listening. Children find the concept of whole body listening fun and engaging. Learning to "listen with your hands" (quiet in your lap or at your side) or "listen with your feet" (stationary, not moving) is a different approach to teaching this important social concept. Sometimes kids may be listening with their ears, but their head is turned away, their body may be fidgety, or their eye gaze may be elsewhere. Behaviors like this send a nonverbal message to others that the child is not listening and part of the group.

6 Expected and Unexpected

Once we have introduced and are beginning to establish the first five core Social Thinking concepts, we move on to the second set of vocabulary words. These concepts are more complex and incorporate and build upon the key ideas taught in the first five lessons. The initial concepts lay a foundation for thinking about and relating to others: when we're in a group we are thinking with our eyes, putting our body in the group, using whole body listening and following the group plan. As a result, children begin to learn that in every social situation a range of behaviors are appropriate/inappropriate. We use the Social Thinking vocabulary "expected" and "unexpected" to steer away from the more traditional "good/bad" behavior language commonly used with students, and also to silently remind them that the perspectives of others are involved in every social encounter we face.

Doing what is expected means understanding that a supplemental range of unstated or "hidden rules" exist in every situation. The hidden rules are those that are implicit in the social setting but are never explicitly taught. For example, nobody tells you that you need to wait for the teacher to look at you before it is your turn to talk. Neurotypical kids just figure this out. To do what is expected, we have to think with our eyes, figure out the group plan and the rules based on the context of the situation, and then follow them. If we do this, we keep other people feeling good about us; in turn this helps us feel good about ourselves. Doing what is unexpected means saying or doing things that do not follow the set of rules, hidden or stated, in the environment.

It is important to teach children that we all have the ability to CHANGE our actions. When we change our behavior to do what is expected, it affects the thoughts and feelings of others about us, hopefully for the better. With social learning, the emphasis has to be on changing someone's thoughts (through your actions) rather than always doing the "expected" behaviors. As educators, our goal is to help children understand that social thinking is more than just choosing the "right" (expected) behavior. Rather than focus on behavior, we focus our children's attention on thinking – about the thoughts, reactions, and feelings in others when we are in their presence. In doing so we give children the tools to participate in the back-and-forth flow of social interaction that can change at any minute!

7 Smart Guess/Wacky Guess

When we want to know something but don't necessarily have all the facts, we can gather lots of clues. When we have some clues, but don't have all of them, we can make a "smart guess." To make a smart guess we think with our eyes, listen to what is happening around us, and combine that with what we already know. We can make smart guesses about what will happen next in a story, what other people are thinking and feeling and what, based on the group plan, we might be expected to do. We use smart guesses when learning new information or trying to figure out how to play or get along with others. Words like "I think…"or "maybe…" let others know we are making a smart guess.

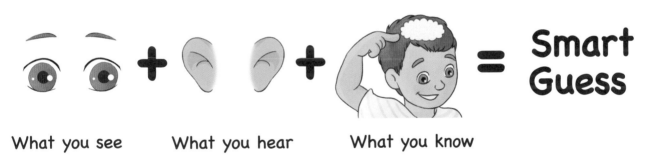

What you see **What you hear** **What you know**

(This concept is adapted from, and discussed in more detail, in the book, *You Are a Social Detective*, by Michelle Garcia Winner and Pamela Crooke. Available at www.socialthinking.com.)

We make a "wacky guess" when we have too little or no information (clues) to help us figure out the situation. If our guess is wrong, it's okay (and even expected!) because we didn't have clues to help us! If you don't think with your eyes, listen to what is happening around you or use what you already know, you might make a wacky guess.

For example: Every morning students come into the class, put away their backpacks and sit down for circle time. A student making a smart guess would gather clues combining what he sees (peers sitting in circle), what he hears ("Time for circle"), and what he already knows (every day I put away my backpack and go to circle) to follow the plan. If the student runs to play with the trains instead, he has made a wacky guess about the expected behavior in the situation and either missed or neglected to consider the clues at hand: everyone else sitting in circle and the daily classroom routine.

Embedded in the concept of smart and wacky guesses is the idea of ***knowing***. To know something means we have gathered sufficient information from what we saw, what we heard and what we already knew. It is easy to know facts; it is more complicated when we add other people and thoughts and feelings into the social equation. For example, if we make the plan, then we know what it is. If someone else makes the plan, we can only make smart guesses about it, unless they tell us what it is. Understanding the distinction between thinking and knowing and actively teaching this to our children will help them learn when to ask for help (because they don't know) and when to make smart social choices based on information they can gather from the situation.

8 Flexible versus Stuck Thinking

"Flexible thinking" is being able to consider different options and strategies to adapt across places and people in the moment. We teach children that we can change our plan, change what we are thinking or give up what we want based on the plan of the group. This is the opposite of "stuck thinking," which is being unable to change what we are doing or thinking based on what is happening around us. For example, if a child always sits on the red square during circle, she would be demonstrating stuck thinking if she could not sit on another colored square when the red one was already occupied. Solving interpersonal problems, learning as a group and being able to maintain one's friendships all require the ability to think flexibly and on occasion change your plan based on the will of the group.

9 Size of the Problem

The size of the problem is a self-regulatory concept we use to teach our students to monitor their behavior and reactions and make appropriate adjustments. It is about helping them learn about putting personal problems in perspective and ties back to expected/unexpected behaviors. We start by teaching children that problems come in all sizes, from big problems to little problems. Once children understand this they are ready to learn that reactions need to match the size of the problem. When our big problems get big reactions and small problems get small ones, that behavior is expected. It is unexpected when children have big reactions to small problems, or small reactions to big problems.

10 *Sharing an Imagination*

The final Social Thinking concept we teach students in this series is about "sharing an imagination." Often our students have a strong singular imagination but they struggle when the situation requires them to share an imagination with others. Sharing an imagination is at the basis of play and conversation. To fully engage in creative and interactive play, we need to be able to imagine what others may be thinking as well as let them in on our own thoughts. This allows us to share an idea, so we can create and sustain play with contributions from all of the play partners. To share an imagination, we have to coordinate our own ideas, goals, and interests with those of another person to pursue a common plan. Just like our five preschoolers demonstrated in our opening scenario, shared imagination is the thread that ties the play experience together and keeps it intact.

Interpreting Difficult Behavior Through the Lens of Social Thinking

Behavior is a near-constant focal point for most adults who work with children in a teaching setting. Many times those of us who know and love young learners reach a breaking point in our patience. Despite that tool bag of strategies we constantly use, there are days when we just cannot tolerate one more tantrum, one more inflexible meltdown, or one more refusal to do what is asked of the group. While it is tempting to view this as "bad behavior" in a child and resort to behavior-based strategies to "eliminate" whatever it is the child should not be doing, we urge you to stop, think and reinterpret the behavior with an eye to what it means to have a social cognitive weakness.

Behavior doesn't manifest in a vacuum; it is the end result of many factors that include our children's abilities, processing styles, sensory regulation systems, and various environmental factors. These factors include our own abilities, teaching and processing styles, our own feelings and perceptions, as well as the influences we exert in the situation based on our personal profile.

Our children with social learning challenges are not intentionally and willfully missing clues, stepping outside the group plan, or melting into tears over a broken crayon. Their social brain doesn't have the hard wiring that allows them to learn in the way other children do. So we ask you to start looking at the actions and reactions of your students through the lens of a social thinking challenge rather than through the traditional behavior lens.

To follow are some common scenarios found in preschools and early elementary settings. We are well aware that life (and the conceptual lens through which we view life) is not as neat and clean as the ideas that follow suggest. We also know that many of the behaviors presented below can be attributed to the combined effect of several areas of social developmental weakness. We believe it is important to see that difficult behavior in young children is a *symptom* of underlying differences in perception, understanding, and ability. The chart is meant to draw attention to the connection between the behavior we notice and the social thinking struggles children may face. In doing so we can decide how best to help our students through their challenges and tailor our teaching accordingly.

Situation	Behavior Lens (leads to a symptomatic fix of a singular action)	Social Thinking Lens (leads to a discovery of social cognitive concepts to teach)
Joshua knocks over Sasha's blocks while waving a fishing toy and laughs even though Sasha is clearly angry.	Joshua is thoughtless and clumsy and doesn't care that Sasha is very upset; results in the teacher telling him to stop the behavior.	Joshua has a hard time self-regulating and reading the facial expressions of others. He does not recognize Sasha is mad or that he is the cause. He needs help with recognizing the thoughts and feelings of others. Teaching the social concepts result in his ability to monitor his body in space and read Sasha's reaction when occasional accidents occur.
The teacher flickers the lights and every child but Rachel moves to the carpet squares for circle time.	Rachel is misbehaving and needs to be taught to follow the rules.	Rachel has not intuited the hidden rules of the classroom and has a hard time thinking with her eyes to observe the expected behavior when the lights are flickered. She needs to follow the group plan.
Jayden interrupts constantly during circle time and answers every question the teacher poses.	Jayden is rude; the other children wait for their turn to talk	Jayden needs to learn whole body listening, thinking with his eyes, and how to follow the group plan.
Olivia wanders the classroom often walking between two people playing or speaking. Or she is off into her own space without regard to the other kids. She leaves the circle before it is time, in the middle of playing with peers and on occasion turns her back in the middle of a project	Olivia is rude and self involved and does not care about her peers.	Olivia needs to learn to think with her eyes, keep her body in the group, and use her social detective tools to figure out the hidden rules of social interaction in the classroom setting.

Situation	Behavior Lens (leads to a symptomatic fix of a singular action)	Social Thinking Lens (leads to a discovery of social cognitive concepts to teach)
Simon melts down when his pencil breaks or someone wants the toy he was planning to use. He may also shrug off the very real upset of a peer in response to something he has done, because he just doesn't "see" the problem.	Simon is overly sensitive to his own needs but insensitive to the feelings of others.	Simon needs to recognize the size of the problem, the emotions of others, and adjusting his own responses appropriately.
Ben never wants to go out to the playground with the class and once he is out there, he does not want to go back in. His mother reports it is impossible to get him out the door to school in the morning.	Ben is inflexible and unable to follow directions.	Ben may have some executive functioning challenges and is caught up in stuck thinking. He needs to be taught how to be more flexible.

Curriculum Overview

The Incredible Flexible You curriculum aligns with the individual storybooks and provides teachers and parents with concrete lessons, fun activities, and ideas for infusing daily interactions with the Social Thinking Vocabulary.

Target Ages and Population

The Incredible Flexible You is targeted to children four to seven years old with social learning weaknesses. It can also be used in regular education classrooms with all children to establish a common vocabulary to talk about social issues and to build social awareness and social smarts. It is a language-based approach and therefore is best suited for children having normal to near normal language development (syntax and semantics) for their age. Not all children with social learning challenges fit this description. Some may have serious language delays or communication disorders and in that case their language will not support them in the process of learning about others.

This curriculum is not well-suited for children who are not yet verbal or whose primary means of communication is echolalia (echoed speech). It may be that young children who are very language delayed eventually become older children with stronger language and learning skills, at which point the Social Thinking concepts and strategies might be a welcome tool to use. Children who do not yet have a solid foundation of joint attention skills or are unable to stay connected to a group are also not good candidates for this curriculum. It is recommended that they first receive individual work in foundational areas through relationship development interventions.

Students who will benefit from this approach may have a range of diagnostic labels, such as High-Functioning Autism, PDD-NOS, Asperger's Syndrome, Nonverbal Learning Disability, Social Communication Disorder, and Attention-Deficit/Hyperactivity Disorder (ADHD). There are also many children, especially at this young age, who have not yet received a diagnostic label or do not quite "fit" diagnostic criteria that would benefit from this introduction to Social Thinking vocabulary. The curriculum is ideal for use with neurotypical students; they will find these lessons fun and a means to enhance their own social learning experience.

However, beware that diagnostic labels alone **do not** determine if this curriculum will be useful to the child. There is a wide range of language functioning and cognitive learning abilities for students labeled with any of the disorders mentioned above. In our work with students, we don't decide if this curriculum is relevant for a child based on the label alone. Instead, we observe and learn about the child as an individual.

If your child/student is a good candidate for these lessons, we hope you enjoy learning about the social process with them!

Grouping

The lessons in this curriculum were designed to teach students with social learning challenges in a small group format (two to four students) to maximize opportunities to address individual needs. With four children, it is ideal to have two adults working together with the children. If you are using the curriculum in a regular class with neurotypical learners, a larger group will be fine as they won't need as much individualized instruction and they will likely move through the concepts more quickly.

One of the key aspects to teaching social thinking is having the flexibility to take advantage of "teachable moments" that occur within the context of the group. For example, a student may come into the room and have a difficult time choosing a carpet square to sit on. If the color they usually choose is not available, a stuck moment may occur! With a low ratio of students, the educator is able to make that a teaching moment, and discuss how to help our brains become more flexible! The moment could easily be lost, however, with a larger group and when teaching priorities are more about group management than teaching to individual needs. From a very practical point of view: our students are receiving social support and instruction because they don't intuitively know how to learn in a group and consider the thoughts and feelings of others! No matter how "bright" they are when learning information on their own, you want to have ample opportunities to teach to their social needs. Plan your group size accordingly as much as is possible.

That said, we realize that education is not always ideal and situations exist where these lessons will need to be adapted to a larger learning group. We encourage educators to think about ways to extend the learning into the classroom at-large.

How to Use the Book

The Incredible Flexible You curriculum is comprised of ten lessons that teach the following Social Thinking Vocabulary concepts adapted for the early learner. Lessons are presented in the following order:

Volume 1
1. Thinking Thoughts and Feeling Feelings
2. The Group Plan
3. Thinking With Your Eyes
4. Body in the Group
5. Whole Body Listening

Volume 2
6. Expected and Unexpected
7. Smart Guess/Wacky Guess
8. Flexible Thinking versus Stuck Thinking
9. Size of the Problem
10. Sharing an Imagination

Each of the lessons is designed to teach a specific Social Thinking concept. The vocabulary builds upon itself; the ideas are not discreet session to session. Once a concept is introduced, it is infused across all the other lessons during relevant moments. It is not expected for students to master a concept after just one lesson. Instead, you will find that deeper levels of understanding will evolve in your students as you use the curriculum at school across the day, and especially when the vocabulary is incorporated beyond the lesson at home by the child's caregivers.

It is recommended that educators read through the entire curriculum before teaching its parts. Social learning is not static; it evolves over time and through experience. Therefore, the curriculum is designed to be taught starting with Lesson 1 and working through the other lessons in order. However, the pacing and movement within a lesson and from lesson to lesson will depend on how quickly your students absorb the ideas, the frequency of sessions week by week, and the amount of time devoted to practicing the Social Thinking concepts within individual classrooms.

It is important to understand that most lessons will take more than one "session" to teach. In some instances you will find it possible to complete the lesson in one or two sessions. For some groups and concepts, you may find yourself working through a lesson over the course of a couple of weeks. Let your students' progress guide your way.

We are aware that there are a variety of school settings where therapy models range from push in to pull out and everything in between. We also realize that members of our audience may range from private therapists who have a one hour session to educators in a school setting who have only 20 minutes (or less!) for running a social thinking group. And, it is our hope that general education teachers will recognize the value of infusing Social Thinking Vocabulary into everyday teaching with their entire classroom. No matter your setting or time constraints, the lesson plans are designed to be flexible. We encourage you to take your time with all of the lessons and teach for social understanding rather than to some specific timetable or calendar goal. With the preschool and early-elementary-aged learner, repetition is always crucial, regardless of the concept. Remember, good social learning is a slow and deep process and your students with social learning challenges have to learn cognitively what their neurotypical peers learned intuitively!

Assessing Your Students' Progress

The rubric below is designed to help you observe your students and assess their understanding and application of each of the concepts. Specific bullet points for each vocabulary concept are included in each lesson in the Take Away Points section. Please be aware of developmental expectations when rating your students and consider that children with language learning weaknesses may have a harder time attaching to the linguistic aspects of the vocabulary but may indeed be able to demonstrate use of the terms.

0 =	No understanding of the concept. They are not using the vocabulary or demonstrating any of the requisite associated behaviors.
1 =	Emerging awareness of the concept. May be able to point out or give examples of its use or misuse on others but are not demonstrating its use even with maximum support and cuing.
2 =	Emerging awareness of the concept. May be able to point out or give examples of its use or misuse on others and are demonstrating its use with support and cuing.
3 =	Solid understanding of the concept and can demonstrate its use with moderate cues.
4 =	Solid understanding of the concept and may be starting to use it with minimal cues.
5 =	Solid understanding of the concept and can demonstrate its use with minimal cues.

If you rate a student at 0 on the majority of the bullet points, consider:
The appropriateness of curriculum for this student.

If you rate a student at 1 or 2 on the majority of the bullet points, consider:
Spending more time teaching this concept before moving on to the next lesson. Explore it in different ways and across settings.

If you rate a student at 3 or above on the majority of the bullet points, consider:
Continuing to use the concept in context and teachable moments as you move forward in teaching the next lesson or deepening knowledge on this one.

Ideas for Writing Goals

At the end of each lesson it is important to take some time to think back through your students' social awareness and responses and assess their abilities in the areas covered by the lesson and those that follow it. If you have gotten this far in the book, you may now realize, or you may already KNOW, that social thinking and social functioning is complex, multifaceted and multidimensional. We suggest the use of a rubric, as a goal with strict performance objectives does not lend itself to the type of flexible social thinking we are hoping to impart to our students.

The sample goals included in Appendix D are written with a rubric assessment format. It would not be possible for us to list every concept, skill and behavior which can be targeted for treatment. Use these as a reference to help you organize your perceptions and observations to create accomplishable goals tailored to each individual child.

Using The Incredible Flexible You Music CD

The Incredible Flexible You music CD is an integrated add-on to the storybooks and curriculum. The CD is a collection of 12 songs developed by Tom Chapin, a GRAMMY® award winning singer/songwriter and Phil Galdston, a GRAMMY nominated songwriter/producer, designed to amplify, augment and reinforce the concepts in each of the storybooks and associated lessons. In many lessons we offer specific suggestions for using the accompanying song as part of our Structured Activities. We encourage you to introduce the songs in the ways suggested but then use and enjoy them as you would any other music. Play the songs during lunch, times of transition, free time and as the children are packing up to go home. Music is motivating and effective! Research on the use of music within therapy supports increased engagement on the part of the listener! Use of the CD will encourage and enhance retention of the Social Thinking Vocabulary as well as offer an entertaining way to revisit and highlight important concepts.

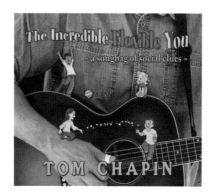

Lesson Layout

Each lesson follows a similar format as outlined below. This section provides additional start-up instructions and some tips and suggestions for teaching the vocabulary concepts.

Social Thinking Concept Targeted

Identifies the Social Thinking Vocabulary the lesson is designed to teach.

Definition

A short definition of the concept, suitable to be shared with children.

Why Do We Teach This Concept?

Outlines why the concept is important in the overall framework of teaching Social Thinking to preschool and early-elementary-aged children.

Before Teaching the Lesson

Bulleted step-by-step reminders for teaching the lesson.

Prepare Materials for Activities

Description of items and prep work needed prior to reading the storybooks and teaching the lesson and activities to children.

Opening Routine

The purpose of the opening routine is to have a consistent signal that group is starting. It sets the stage for preparing the children to think about each other and the plan for the day. In this way, students know what to expect when they start group each time you meet. This predictability can make a big difference in increasing participation and reducing anxiety.

Before your first session you will need to prepare a few materials for use in each opening group routine. *Take photographs of the children in the group and laminate them for durability.* You will be using these each session!

How to do the Opening Routine:

1. Before students arrive:
   - Draw a large thought bubble on your white or black board or a piece of paper.
   - Write out the schedule or plan for the day; pair with a visual. (Find samples to use in the Appendix.) You can also take photographs, download pictures from the Internet, or draw stick figures.

2. Once students enter the room, instruct them to find a spot to sit and put their "bodies in the group." We find carpet squares, foam pieces, or child-sized chairs are all helpful in defining individual spaces.

3. Once everyone is seated, take out the envelope with the students' photographs.

4. Tell the children, "Let's find out who is in our group today."

5. Pull out one photograph and show it to the group. Once all have seen the photo, greet that child. This is a great opportunity to talk about what's expected when we say "hi" to someone we know (we look at the person to show we are thinking about him or her, use our words or wave, turn our bodies toward him or her). Be sure to also discuss how greeting someone makes that person feel happy and included in the group.

6. After the group has greeted that child, the student can place the photograph below the thinking bubble. Using the student's name say, "_____ is in the group and ready to think about the plan." As children become more familiar with this routine, encourage them to use the vocabulary when they place their picture. For example, "I am part of the group and ready to think about the plan."

7. Follow the same routine for each child. In the end, all children present should have their photos below the thought bubble.

8. Next, share the plan for the day. In the end, your board should look similar to this:

Introduce the Vocabulary using The Incredible Flexible You Storybooks

Each of the storybooks focuses on one Social Thinking Vocabulary concept. The text and illustrations provide a framework to teach the concept, model the vocabulary and language, and provide opportunities for practice.

How to Use the Storybooks:

1. Start with the Cover
    Before you open the story, take some time to look at the cover illustration and help your group make some "smart guesses" about the story. It's okay to use the smart guess vocabulary before you have formally introduced the smart guess concept (storybook 7). Doing so provides early exposure, an illustration of the concept in context, and practice. Point out important information or clues to help determine what the story is going to be about, such as:

    - Where are the characters? What is the setting/context?
    - Who is there?
    - What are they thinking?
    - How are they feeling?
    - What are they doing?
    - What is their plan? What might they do next?

2. Teaching Moments and Break Out Activities
    The stories are intended to be interactive and engage children in the learning process. Throughout the story you will find icons on the bottom of some of the pages that prompt teaching moments that go beyond what is written in the story text.

    Icons are as follows:

    The Stop and Notice icon is a prompt to pause and highlight extra information on the page that is not explicitly stated in the text.

    Examples include:

    - Draw attention to the concept within the illustration. For example, in the *Body in the Group* story (storybook 4), stop and notice that the school of fish have their bodies in the group while the octopuses do not.
    - Notice facial expressions as clues to how characters are feeling and what they might be thinking.
    - Point out vocabulary that has been previously introduced in the story: "He has his body in the group!"

The Stop and Discuss teaching moments allow the educator to delve deeper into what the students are learning by asking children to participate in a discussion. They also provide opportunities to draw on prior knowledge and previous experiences.

Examples include:

- Smart guesses about what characters are thinking and feeling or going to do next.
- Talk about why a character feels a certain way.
- In *The Group Plan* story (storybook 2), stop and discuss why Ellie was feeling upset when another child wasn't following the plan.

When you see the Stop and Do icon it is time to get up and put the concept into action! These are break out activities designed to take you away from the story while continuing to reinforce the concepts being taught. For instance, in the *Thinking Thoughts and Feeling Feelings* story (storybook 1), one Stop and Do activity is to act out part of the story.

Instructions for each of the Stop and Do activities are provided within the lesson. These are engaging and fun opportunities to enrich and expand upon what your students are learning.

3. Structured Activities
   These are games, activities, and songs from the music CD used outside of the story reading to reinforce and put the Social Thinking concepts into action.

4. Dramatic Play: Reinforcing the Concept and Vocabulary
   Sharing an imagination is at the heart of play and conversation. When we engage in creative and interactive play, we often imagine what others may be thinking. This allows us to share an idea in our heads so we can create and sustain play with contributions from all of the play partners. To share an imagination, you have to coordinate your ideas, goals and interests with those of another person to pursue a common plan. Our students may have wonderful creative ideas and imaginations of their own, but the difficulty comes because they can't figure out how to share in an idea if it is not their own.

The Dramatic Play section provides specific examples for using the concepts outside of the lesson itself during less structured play time. This is where your children will have the opportunity to use the vocabulary and the concepts during real time interactions with other students as they practice sharing an imagination.

During dramatic play we also introduce the idea of the three parts of play: set up, play, and clean up. We teach children this sequence so they understand that collaborative play involves more than just the "doing." When we play with others, there is a set up phase where we define what it is we will be doing and make sure that everyone's ideas are considered. That is what makes it collaborative. Second, we engage in the actual playing. The third and final part is clean up. We include this because staying involved in interactions to their logical conclusion is an important aspect of executive function and accomplishing one's goals.

Set Up

Have children share their ideas to come up with a group plan:
- What do we know about _____(theme for the day)?
- What materials will we need?
- What do we know about what people might say and do?
- Once the group has brainstormed ideas, it is time to play.

Play

Depending on your group's exposure to the concept and their learning pace, you will go in one of following directions with your group:
- The first time you introduce a concept, the teacher chooses activities and everyone follows that plan.
- Later, they can take turns following each person's plan.
- Finally the group can decide on a plan together by compromising and negotiating. With our youngest and least adept students this might mean just mushing their ideas together into a whole. Later, it might be reaching some degree of real consensus but keep in mind: some groups may not reach this stage of collaborative play for a very long time.

Challenges with pretend play can be based on many of our students' core challenges that include literal, black and white thinking, mental rigidity, or an inability to consider another person's point of view. These students may shut down, withdraw, refuse, declare that the props they are using are balls and not pretend apples, that the girl two feet away is in your classroom and not under the water and that she is certainly not a mermaid! To follow are some ideas that might help you through those challenging moments.

- Help them be part of the group even if they can't share in the play plan or the imagination yet.

- Help them observe what peers are doing as they play: what are they doing, what are they saying, and what might they be thinking?
- Make it visual—provide context through pictures and play materials.
- Provide more concrete, representational play materials if needed. For instance, use play food, such as a plastic apple, in place of pretending a picture of an apple or a red ball is an apple.
- Give them specific ideas about how they can participate. Spend time talking and thinking about what they can do and say to be part of the plan.

Clean Up

Clean up is a very important part of play for many reasons. First, as we noted earlier, it is an important executive function skill to be able to participate in the planning, execution and follow up of any activity. Second, it is a great time to reinforce the concept of working together: everybody decides what to play together, everybody plays and then everybody cleans up as a group. Finally completing all three parts of play together means we are following the group plan.

Closing Routine

As with the opening routine, it is also important to have a consistent end to each teaching session. The closing activity signals the group is coming to an end and prepares the students for another transition. It also provides an opportunity to highlight how the children in the group participated successfully and gave other people good thoughts about them.

How to Do the Closing Routine:
- Instruct students to bring their bodies back to the group and find a seat.
- Provide a quick summary statement of the day. For example, "Today in group we learned how to listen with our whole bodies."
- Give positive and specific feedback to each child about something that child did to make you have good thoughts. For example, "Joe brought his body to the group right away. Jane was thinking with her eyes. Kyle followed the plan during the dinosaur game. Tres was flexible when it was time to stop playing trains."
  - As you give the positive feedback, hold the thought bubble prop over your head to signify you are having thoughts about each child.
  - *Note: We know (and have definitely experienced) many times when students in the group did NOT give us good thoughts! We are choosing to address the positive moments for several reasons. It is important to set a positive tone with this vocabulary. In our experience, when children repeatedly hear negative feedback, they begin to attach negative feelings to the vocabulary terms. By contrast, if the "flexible" and positive moments are highlighted, they feel initial success and will be more open to learning about the*

more difficult moments later on. Also, when children hear positive feedback about their behavior they are often able to repeat it!

○ If you find yourself in a situation where a student has had a very tough day—and this does happen–attempt to find a redeeming moment. This is not to say the difficult times should be ignored. It is important to talk through this and set an expectation for behavior that contributes to the group plan. Attempt to focus, however, more on what they did to change your thoughts during that tough time.

● Have the group say "goodbye" to each student (modeling the expected way to do so) as you take his or her picture off the board and place it back in the envelope.

Beyond the Lesson: Generalize the Vocabulary to Other Settings

Just because the lesson is over doesn't mean the learning stops! In this section, you will find suggestions for how to continue to use the vocabulary beyond the structured lesson. Keep in mind, the Social Thinking Vocabulary is intended to be used across a child's day at home, during school, and in the community. Social thinking happens everywhere!

Take Away Points for the Lesson

Included in this section is the rubric discussed on page Q in the curriculum, accompanied by specific key core concepts we want students to take away from the lesson. You can use these points to assess your student's knowledge and determine whether more time and teaching is needed on the concept or whether the student is ready to move on to the next Social Thinking lesson.

The Family Letter: Extending Learning Outside the Classroom

This section includes an introduction to the curriculum and a family letter for each concept that can be copied and sent home to extend learning across the school-home setting. It provides an explanation of the Social Thinking concept, its importance, as well as activities and suggestions on how to practice the vocabulary at home. It can be copied directly from the materials CD or modified to include individual observations or specific group activities.

Thinking Thoughts and Feeling Feelings

Social Thinking Concept Targeted

What is a thought? What is a feeling?

Definition

Your brain is your thought maker. We define a thought as an idea, picture, or quiet words you have in your brain.

Your heart is your feelings keeper. We define a feeling as something that happens in your body. To help us talk about our feelings we use words like *happy, sad, mad*, and *scared*.

Why Do We Teach this Concept?

Social learning is all about thoughts and feelings. The ability to think about others, play collaboratively and establish friendships involves thoughts: knowing our own, sharing them with others and taking others' thoughts into account as we act and react. We introduce these concepts first because all subsequent Social Thinking concepts and vocabulary lessons are tied back to thoughts. (What are you thinking? What am I thinking? What is the group thinking about?) We make the connection to feelings because what we think and what we feel are inseparably linked.

In exploring thoughts and feeling, we begin by establishing a connection to body parts. Young learners know we all have many body parts and each part has a job to do. For example, we can see hands clap and feet jump and run. We then connect that information to the more abstract concepts of thoughts and emotions. That is, there are other parts inside our bodies that have important jobs too. Our brain and heart are two of those parts we use when we are around people. Our brain is our thought maker; our heart is our feelings keeper.

Before Teaching the Lesson

- Read through the Lesson Plan and the Teaching Moment activities associated with it.
- Read through the storybook, noting the different places to Stop and Do, Stop and Notice, and/or Stop and Discuss.
- Read through the different Structured Activities to be done within the lesson.
- Prepare materials: create props, gather toys, print out images, etc. for the different activities.
- Familiarize yourself with the lyrics to the song used in teaching the lesson.
- Review the core concepts and rubric in the Take Away Points section of the lesson.
- Review the goal suggestions for this concept. (Find goals for all lessons in Appendix D.)

Prepare Materials for Stop and Do Activities

(Find all templates at the end of the lesson, in Appendix A, and on the materials CD at the end of this book.)

Page 7. Dice Roll: What Can Your Body Do?
Assemble dice:
- Cut out body part cards using template provided in Appendix A.
- Attach cards to each side of a large square block.
- Alternative suggestion:
  - Use a Mr. Potato Head toy and pull out individual body parts.
  - Place body parts or individual cards into an opaque bag to be drawn out one by one.

Create Talking Bubble Props
Cut out talking bubble using template. Transfer to heavy cardstock or laminate to make it more durable.

Page 11. Create Thought Bubble Props
(Note: You will use these props in future lessons as well!)

Teacher's thought bubble (one per adult working with the group)
- Cut out thought bubble using template (find all templates in Appendix A). Transfer to heavy cardstock or laminate to make it more durable.
- Affix thought bubble to ruler or stick.
- Add Velcro® strip or dots. (You will be attaching various images within the thought bubble from time to time.)

Thought bubbles for children (one per child)
- Cut out thought bubbles using template. Transfer to heavy cardstock or laminate to make them more durable.
- Attach thought bubbles to popsicle sticks.

Page 13. "Where You Think a Thought" Music Activity

- Prep music player to track 1.
- Preview lyrics (Appendix B).

Page 15. *I'm Thinking of Something…Find It Game*

- If you haven't already created a thought bubble prop, do so now.
- Gather red, blue, yellow, and green paper.
- Cut into squares small enough to fit inside your thought bubble prop.
- Locate items (in corresponding colors) around the room.

Pages 22-25

Gather following props:
- Bubbles for blowing
- Spider (puppet, toy, or picture)
- Paper with artwork (drawing) on it. (Something that can be torn in half.)
- Ice cream cone (toy or picture: scoop of ice cream must be able to be separated from cone)

"Show Me What You're Feeling" Music Activity

- Prep music player to track 2.
- Preview lyrics (Appendix B).

Prepare Materials for Structured Activities

What do They Like to Think About? Fun with Familiar Characters

- Find images or photographs of things you (the teacher) like to do and think about.
- Find images, stuffed animals, or toys of three to four familiar characters from books, movies, or television. The more your students know about these characters the better.
- Find images of things each of these characters might like to think about. For example, the Hungry Caterpillar likes to think about food. Ernie from Sesame Street likes to think about his rubber duck. Attach Velcro to the back of each image. In the activity you will affix these images to your thought bubble prop.

You're Having a Thought!

- Gather various props to use as examples. Those mentioned in the activity include a bucket, a hula-hoop and a book. You can use others.

"Show Me What You're Feeling" Music Activity

- Prep music player to track 2.
- Preview lyrics (Appendix B).

Thinking or Talking Activity

Gather materials (common objects) and place in a bag

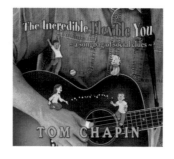

Lesson Plan ❶

Story Summary

Meet Evan, Ellie, Jesse and Molly, the main characters who appear in *The Incredible Flexible You* series. In this first story, *Thinking Thoughts and Feeling Feelings*, we learn all about two important concepts: thoughts and feelings.

The Lesson Flow

- Opening routine. (See page 42 in Introduction for more details.)
- Read the story, using the Teaching Moment suggestions included.
- Do Structured Activities.
- Reinforce the concept and vocabulary during the Dramatic Play activity.
- Closing routine. (See page 47 in Introduction for more details.)
- Send Family Letter home (Appendix C).

Teaching Moments - *Thinking Thoughts and Feeling Feelings*

Stop and Do

Page 7

Dice Roll: What Can Your Body Do?

Before beginning this activity, show your students the pictures on the dice of the various body parts. When you show the image of the mouth, bring out your talking bubble prop. Then show the illustration of Jesse in the storybook (page 7) and explain that when we see talking bubbles, it means words are coming out of someone's mouth. In this illustration, Jesse is using his mouth to talk, so we see a talking bubble.

Roll one of the dice. The face up body part will be your focus. Point to the body part on yourself and give a few examples of what you can do with it. For example:

"I use my feet to walk, run, and jump." Then have your group do those actions together. "Now let's all use our feet to jump. Now let's all make our feet walk."

Have the children take turns rolling a die and contributing their ideas.

Examples for other body parts include:
- Hands: Throw, draw, build
- Mouth: Eat, talk, sing. (Have your students use the talking bubble prop by putting it next to their mouths when talking.)
- Eyes: Blink, see, look at others
- Ears: Hear, listen

Alternative option: If you do not have block dice to roll, use the individual cards or use toy props. Mr. Potato Head parts, for example, work well. Place the body parts in a bag and have children take turns selecting from the bag.

Page 9

Have your students touch their heads and chests to show where their brains and hearts are located. Talk about how they are inside our bodies.

Page 11

Show your group the thought bubble prop you created.

Page 13

Music Activity. "Where You Think a Thought" (Track 1)

- Hand out thought bubble props to all children.
- Before starting the music, tell your group they will be listening for the word "thought." When they hear this word, they can hold the thought bubble props above their heads.
- Act out lyrics with children as you listen together (clapping hands, tapping toes, etc.). Hold your thought bubble prop up when you hear the word "thought."

Page 15

Point out how every character in the story is thinking about the game and thinking about the other kids while they are together. For example, Evan is thinking about playing the ball game with Ellie, Jesse and Molly. He is thinking about the game and thinking about the other kids in his group. Ellie is thinking about playing the ball game with Evan, Jesse and Molly, etc. Your goal is to introduce the concept that we think about what we are doing while we also think about the people around us.

Game. *I'm Thinking of Something…Find It Game*

To begin, everyone stands up. Hold your thought bubble prop above your head. Place a colored square in the thought bubble and say to the group, "I'm thinking of something (red)." Tell your students to find something (red) and touch it with their hand. For example, one child might touch a red chair, another a red ball. More than one child can touch the same item. When everyone is touching a (red) item say, "We are all thinking about something (red)!" Continue the game with a new color.

Page 16

Ask your students: "What other names for feelings do you know besides happy, sad, mad, and scared?"

Page 20

Discuss the different characters, point to their hearts, and the associated feelings in each character.

Pages 22-25

As you read these pages, use props to act out the scene. Blow bubbles, make a spider puppet or toy crawl around, rip a page of artwork in half, and drop a scoop of toy ice cream on the ground. At each page, ask your students to imagine how they would feel in the situation.

Ask your students to stand up and act out the different feelings together. Encourage them to demonstrate the various facial expressions and body language for each emotion. Please remember that the expectation in this activity is self-awareness, not reading the emotion of another person, out of context. We want our students to think about how their faces and bodies look and feel when they are experiencing an emotion.

Music Activity.
"Show Me What You're Feeling" (Track 2)
Act out lyrics with children as you listen together so the children can practice demonstrating the various feelings with their faces and bodies. If children need help remembering what the different emotions look like, copy pages from the story, use expression/emotion charts or pictures from magazines, etc. and post nearby as a reference during the song.

Page 27

Ask your students: "How can Molly tell that Jesse is mad? What are the clues from his body and face?"

Page 30

Draw the children's attention to each character's own thoughts. How does Evan want to add to the block city? Ellie? Jesse? Molly?

Structured Activities

After you have completed the story and corresponding Teaching Moments, the following activities are used to reinforce the Social Thinking concept. Keep in mind that your purpose is to model the use of the vocabulary during teachable moments.

Draw attention to times when your students are thinking thoughts and feeling feelings. It is important to use the vocabulary at the time you notice children doing the concepts well, so students can pay attention to what they are expected to do. If the vocabulary is used to tell children what not to do ("Cooper is not thinking about my feelings."), then students pair the words with bad behavior and not as a tool through which they can learn positive lessons. As much as possible in this lesson, draw awareness to the idea that we are always having thoughts and feelings.

Activity 1 — What do They Like to Think About? Fun with Familiar Characters

Use the thought bubble prop and pictures of items you like. Hold the thought bubble over your head and tell the group, "There are lots of things I like to think about. I like to read books. I like to think about books." Then select one picture (for example, books) and as you attach it to the thought bubble say, "I like to think about reading books." Then make the connection between thoughts and feelings. "I like to think about reading books. This gives me a happy and calm feeling." Do the same for other pictures of things you like to think about.

Extend the discussion by talking about favorite and familiar characters from books, movies, or television. For example, Ernie likes to think about his rubber duck and the Hungry Caterpillar likes thinking about food. Use your thought bubble prop and hold it above the character's head. Ask your group "What might [the Hungry Caterpillar] like to think about?" If they are having difficulty generating ideas you might show a few choices: "Does the caterpillar like to think about food or his rubber ducky?" Once the group figures out the right answer, put the image in the thought bubble and review, "The caterpillar likes to think about food. This gives him a happy feeling!"

Activity 2 — You are Having a Thought!

The goal of this activity is to raise children's awareness that they are having a thought even when they do not consciously realize it. To draw attention to this internal process, do something unexpected and out of the ordinary!

Start by stacking blocks on your head. As the children observe you doing this unexpected action tell them, "You are having a thought! I'm stacking blocks on my head and that is silly." Then, hold a thought bubble above each child's head and say, "You are having a thought about me!"

Pass out thought bubble props to each child. As you do more unexpected actions, encourage them to hold the thought bubble up and use the vocabulary, "I'm having a thought about you!"

Here are some ideas to get you started but feel free to use your own unexpected examples!

- Take off your shoes, put them on your hands, and clap.
- Wear a bucket as a hat.
- Lie down and pretend to fall asleep; snore even.

- Hula hoop.
- Put a book on your head.
- Do the chicken dance.

Activity 3 — "Show Me What You're Feeling" Music Activity

Use the "Show Me What You're Feeling" song again as an opportunity for further practice and learning. Before playing the music, review with your students how each feeling as described in the story looks on their faces and bodies.

During the instrumental section, choose a student to go into the middle of the circle and act out a feeling. Then all students act out that same feeling.

Note: Many of our students have a difficult time with initiation and generating ideas, especially around the topic of feelings. You might show them visuals of different emotions (pages from the story, for example) so they can choose before taking their turn.

Activity 4 — Thinking or Talking?

Quick review: Show the thought bubble and talking bubble and explain the difference between the two. Thought bubbles show when others are thinking, having pictures or quiet words in their brain. Talking bubbles show when someone is saying something out loud.

First, model the activity for your students. Take out the bag filled with common objects (marker, paper, cup, toy). Tell students: "I've got a bag full of things. I'm going to reach in and take one thing out. I'm going to THINK about that thing. I'm not going to SAY anything. I will keep the words in my brain."

Pull out one object from the bag. Hold your thought bubble prop next to your brain. Put the object in the thought bubble. Then tell students, "I'm thinking about this thing."

Next, take out the talking bubble prop and hold it by your mouth. Tell your students "Now, I'm going to talk about this thing. I found a marker!"

Have the children take turns following your model. Contrast the difference between thinking and talking using the appropriate props.

Dramatic Play: Reinforcing the Concept and Vocabulary

Prepare Materials for Dramatic Play

- Gather images related to building a block city to use as your children talk, brainstorm and plan. For instance, you might gather a set of building blocks and (optional) affix images of storefronts to some of the blocks. Examples might include:
  - Gas station
  - Police station
  - Grocery store
  - Library
  - Fire Station
  - School
- Gather vehicles (cars, trucks, buses) to drive in the city.
- Locate other props to be used in recreating any of the ideas you or the children may generate about building a block city.

Building a Block City

Using the Social Thinking concept and vocabulary during less structured playtime is a perfect opportunity to help children learn to use the vocabulary with their peers and appreciate that we are all having thoughts and feelings all the time.

Set Up

"In our group we read the story about Evan, Ellie, Jesse and Molly and their thoughts and feelings. At the end of the story, they shared a thought of building a block city together. Today we are going to make a block city too! Let's think about a city. What do we know?"

You can use the story illustration to help provide context. Ask children different questions about a city:

- Who lives in a city?
- What places do you see? (Library, park, grocery store, gas stations, houses, apartments, stores, schools)
- How do people get around the city? (Walk, drive, bike, bus, cable car)

As the children brainstorm, place pictures of items in a thought bubble. For example, if one child shares that she sees a school, place the picture of a school in the thought bubble. If a child shares an idea that is not pictured, feel free to draw a quick sketch to visually represent his or her idea and attach it to the thought bubble.

"Together we thought about a city and all the different things we can see and do. Cities are so big, it takes many people to build them. One person can build his or her own house but a whole group of people is needed to build a neighborhood. Let's make a group plan. What type of city should we build together?"

Listen to your students brainstorm ideas for play. Some suggestions include:
- Build roads.
- Build a school, library, gas station, police station, etc.
- Use characters (stuffed animals, play people) to move through and play in the city. Take them to the store, get gas in their car, go to the park, ride the bus.

Once the group has brainstormed ideas, it is time to build the block city and play.

You will go in one of the following directions with your group:
- Teacher chooses activities and everyone follows that plan.
- Take turns following each person's plan.
- Students put their ideas together to make a group plan.*

* Please remember, **some groups may not reach collaborative play for a long time!**

The goal of dramatic play is to illustrate the vocabulary in action. Help your students gain a greater awareness of when they are having thoughts and the feelings that go along with those thoughts.

Throughout play, provide visual supports. Use the thought bubble props whenever you use the vocabulary. For example, hold the thought bubble (with or without an image of blocks in it) above your head when you say, "We are making a block city together. We are thinking about building with blocks!" As play evolves, keep the thought bubble prop nearby. If the group moves from building a library to driving a bus around town, use the thought bubble to illustrate the change in others' thoughts. "Josh is thinking about driving the bus." "We are all thinking about each other while we build our city."

Model the use of the thoughts and feelings vocabulary in the context of the block city dramatic play activities. Consider the following examples:
- "Kyle is thinking about building a police station and Tres is thinking about making a road. They can put their thoughts together and make the road connect to the police station."
- "What are Jane and Joe thinking about right now? Let's look at what they are playing with."
- "How is Phil feeling? Let's look at his face and body."
- "Erik is thinking about building a skyscraper but the blocks keep falling down. He looks like he is feeling mad. His mouth is turned down into a frown."
- "Ryan is helping Erik stack up the blocks. He is thinking about Erik. This makes Erik feel happy. Ryan is feeling good too."

The final part of play is always clean up! Continue to use the vocabulary during this time and encourage students to use their own thought bubbles to show they are thinking about the task and each other. Examples include:

- "I am thinking about cleaning up."
- "Ann is thinking about putting the blocks up on the shelf."
- "Yago is thinking about helping Ann clean up."
- "We are all thinking about cleaning up together. This makes me feel happy!"

Beyond The Lesson: Generalize the Vocabulary to Other Settings

Just because the lesson is over doesn't mean learning stops! Continue to use and reinforce the vocabulary in future lessons and throughout your time together with students. Some suggestions follow.

While getting ready for large group time:
- "It's circle time. I'm thinking about everyone putting their bodies in the group."
- "Gretchen is thinking about sitting on the blue carpet square."
- "Vedant is ready. He is thinking about our group."
- "I'm thinking about reading a book to you all."
- "I see Lisa smiling. She is feeling happy."

Choice time:
- "Megan likes blocks. She is thinking about playing with blocks."
- "Ibrahim does not like play dough. He is thinking about the other choice – doing a puzzle instead."
- "Pablo and Lila are playing cars together. They are smiling and having fun. They are feeling happy and thinking about each other."

When group time is ending:
- "Today in group we played with dinosaurs. We were thinking about dinosaurs."
- "Group time is over now. It's time to think about cleaning up."
- "It's time to think about saying goodbye to each other."
- "We are all done with group time today. Everyone did a great job playing together. You can tell by the smile on my face that I am feeling happy. I am excited to see you again next time."

Take Away Points For This Lesson

On the following page you will find a list of the key core concepts we want students to take away from this lesson. Review the list and assess your student's knowledge based on the rubric below.

0 =	No understanding of the concept. They are not using the vocabulary or demonstrating any of the requisite associated behaviors.
1 =	Emerging awareness of the concept. May be able to point out or give examples of its use or misuse on others but are not demonstrating its use even with maximum support and cuing.
2 =	Emerging awareness of the concept. May be able to point out or give examples of its use or misuse on others and are demonstrating its use with support and cuing.
3 =	Solid understanding of the concept and can demonstrate its use with moderate cues.
4 =	Solid understanding of the concept and may be starting to use it with minimal cues.
5 =	Solid understanding of the concept and can demonstrate its use with minimal cues.

If you rate a student at 0 on the majority of the bullet points, consider:
The appropriateness of curriculum for this student. (See page 36 in introduction.)

If you rate a student at 1 or 2 on the majority of the bullet points, consider:
Spending more time teaching this concept before moving on to the next lesson. Explore it in different ways and across settings.

If you rate a student at 3 or above on the majority of the bullet points, consider:
Continuing to use the concept in context and teachable moments as you move forward in teaching the next lesson or deepening knowledge on this one.

Lesson ❶ Take Away Points for *Thinking Thoughts and Feeling Feelings*

The expectation is for kids to be exposed to (not master) the following concepts:

- Basic information about the Brain
  - They have a body part called a brain.
  - Their brain is inside the head; they can't see it.
  - The brain's job is to think and make thoughts.

- Basic information about the Heart
  - They have a body part called a heart.
  - It is located inside the chest; they can't see it.
  - Our heart is our feelings keeper.

- Information about Thoughts
  - Thoughts are quiet words or pictures in your head.
  - We represent thoughts in illustrations by a thought bubble.
  - We all have thoughts when we are with other people.
  - Other people have thoughts too when they are with us.

- Information about Feelings
  - We can see how others are feeling by what they say, what they do, and how they look.
  - We can observe others' feelings by reading their facial expressions and body language.
  - We take into consideration the context (what is happening around us) to help determine others' feelings.

- After completing this lesson, we want kids to start using words such as *brain, thought, feeling, thinking.*

The Family Letter: Extending Learning Outside the Classroom

As children learn new Social Thinking vocabulary, it is helpful to solicit the help of parents and family members in using the same vocabulary at home.

The family letter for *Thinking Thoughts and Feeling Feelings* includes an activity that gives children additional opportunities to explore the different things they like to think about. Share the letter with families and encourage them to complete the activity at home and return the thought bubble handout next time. Then have children share their work with each other during your next session together.

Find the Family Letter in Appendix C and on the materials CD in the back of this book.

Lesson 1

Thinking Thoughts and Feeling Feelings

Family Letter and At Home Activities

Social learning is all about **thoughts** and **feelings.** The ability to think about others, play collaboratively and establish friendships is all about thoughts; knowing our own, sharing them with others and taking others' thoughts into account as we act and react. We introduce these concepts first because all subsequent concepts and vocabulary lessons are tied back to thoughts. (What are you thinking? What am I thinking? What is the group thinking about?) We make the connection to feelings because what we think and what we feel are inseparable.

In exploring thoughts and feelings, we begin by establishing a connection to body parts. Children are familiar with their bodies and we are able to use what they know: that we all have many body parts and each part has a job to do. In most cases, we can see these parts and watch them do their jobs. For example, we can see hands clap, hold, and touch, and feet tap, jump and run. We then connect that information to the more abstract concepts of thoughts and emotions. That is, there are other parts inside our bodies that have important jobs too. Our brain and heart are two of those parts we use when we are around people. Our brain is our thought maker. We define a thought as an idea, picture, or words you have in your brain. To help us talk about thoughts we use words like *think* and *know*. Our heart is our feelings keeper. A feeling is something we feel in our body. To help us talk about our feelings we use words like *happy, sad, mad,* and *scared.*

In the first story of The Incredible Flexible You™ series, we meet the main characters, Evan, Ellie, Jesse and Molly. These four children go on many adventures to introduce and explore Social Thinking Vocabulary and concepts. In their first adventure, they learn all about two important concepts: thoughts and feelings.

At home, it is important to raise your child's awareness that s/he is having thoughts. We practiced this by drawing attention to examples that were big and exaggerated. When children saw us do something unexpected (out of the ordinary, silly,

Lesson 1. Template 1. Thought Bubble for Teacher

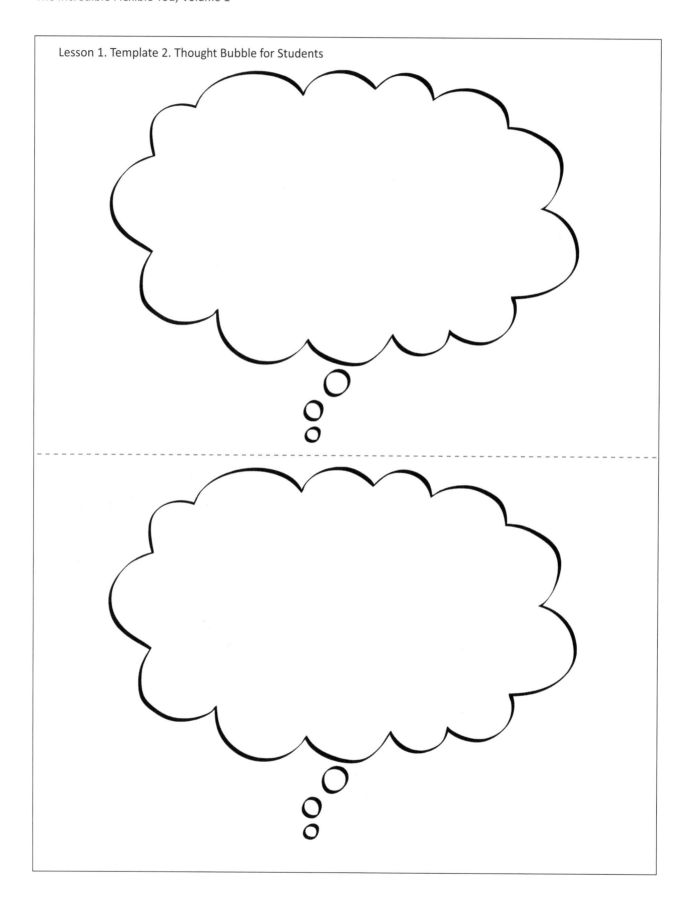

Lesson 1. Template 2. Thought Bubble for Students

Lesson 1. Template 3. Talking Bubble

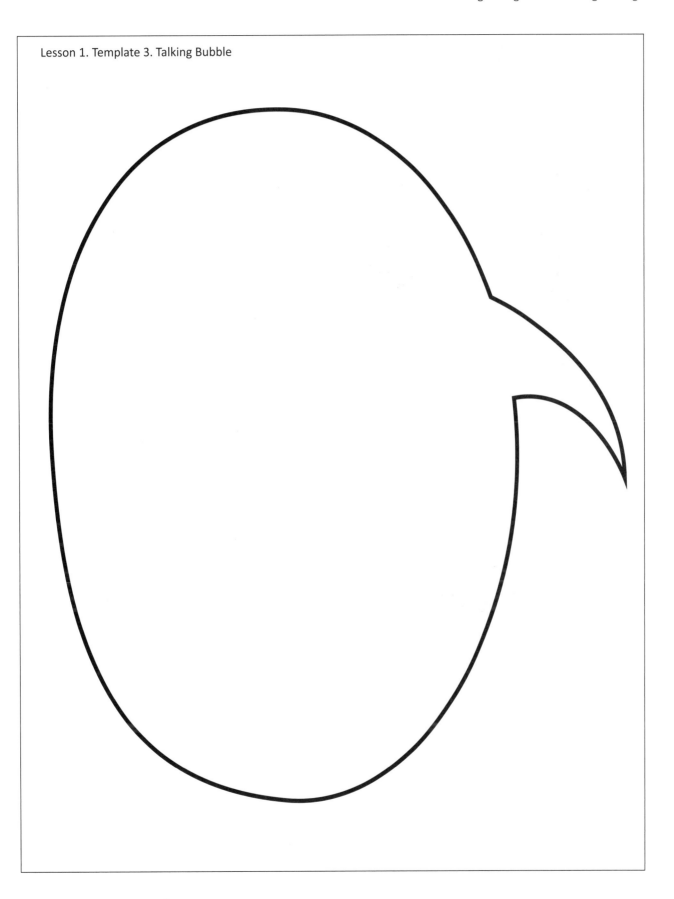

Lesson 1. Template 4. Body Part Cards

Images on template on CD are sized to fit on a 4" preschool block.

Lesson 1. Template 4. Body Part Cards

Images on template on CD are sized to fit on a 4" preschool block.

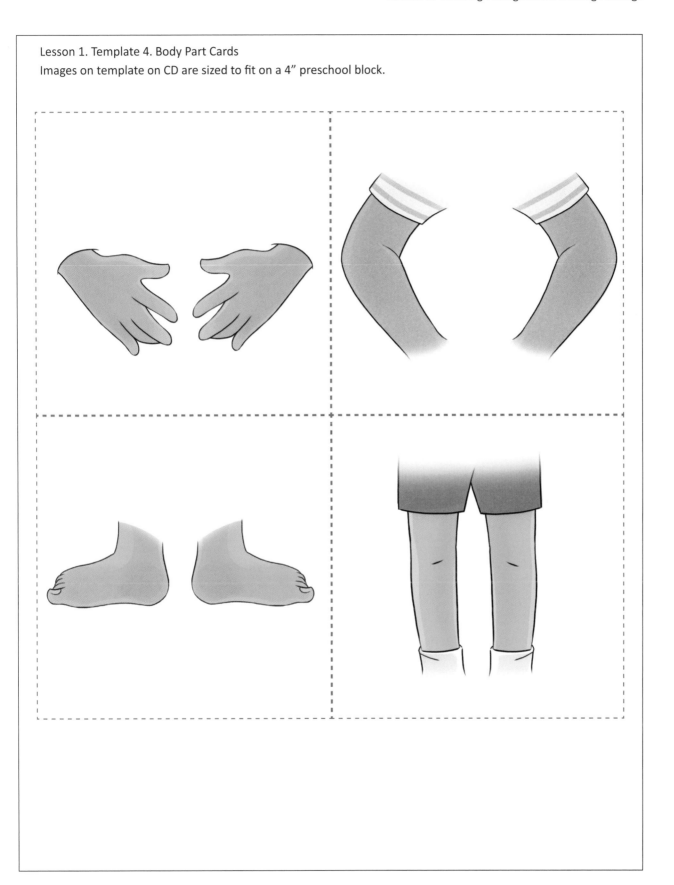

Lesson 2

The Group Plan

Social Thinking Concept Targeted
The Group Plan

Definition
When everyone is thinking about and doing the same thing, it is called *the group plan*. This is in contrast to following one's own plan.

Why Do We Teach this Concept?
We talk about the group plan as a way to help children know what is expected they think about and do when they are part of a group. When everyone is following the plan, we are thinking of each other. This in turn makes everyone feel calm and comfortable. This is in contrast to following one's own plan. When people follow their own plan, others have uncomfortable thoughts and feelings.

It is important to note that the focus of this lesson is to make your students aware they are part of a group and that group has a plan. As the teacher, your role is to label and identify the group plan and to contrast that with following one's own plan. The expectation, at this point, is *not* to have the children "read" the plan of the whole group. To read a plan, children must take clues from what they see, hear, and know about the situation and people in it to figure out what is going on around them. Many students are not ready for this step yet. In fact, we call this concept making a "smart guess" and it is introduced later in the curriculum when children have a more solid foundation of the underlying concepts.

Before Teaching the Lesson

- Read through the Lesson Plan and the Teaching Moment activities associated with it.
- Read through the storybook, noting the different places to Stop and Do, Stop and Notice, and/or Stop and Discuss.
- Read through the different Structured Activities to be done within the lesson.
- Prepare materials: create props, gather toys, print out images, etc. for the different activities.
- Familiarize yourself with the lyrics to the song used in teaching the lesson.
- Review the core concepts and rubric in the Take Away Points section of the lesson.
- Review the goal suggestions for this concept. (Find goals for all lessons in Appendix D.)

Prepare Materials for Structured Activities

Apple Scramble Activity
- Gather approximately 10 "apples."
- You can make apples using the template in Appendix A (cut it out of construction paper) or gather balls of various colors, shapes and sizes to pretend they are apples. You can also use play food for a more realistic prop.
- Find a bucket or basket large enough to fit all the apples.

Milk Pail Obstacle Course
- Gather two pails.
- Set up three obstacles along a simple course. Children will work in pairs or a group of three students to complete obstacles together. Think of this list as a *create-your-own obstacle course menu* – pick and choose the activities that match your children's skill levels and the materials you have on hand. Ideas include:
  - Filling the pail with "milk" (cotton balls, crumpled paper, ping pong balls).
  - Walk over pillows, beanbag chairs, or soft cushions.
  - Set up farm themed stuffed animals on the floor. Walk and weave through the obstacles.
  - Step in and out of hula-hoops.
  - Walk through a "garden" without stepping on "vegetables" or make a pretend pigpen and watch out for the pigs!

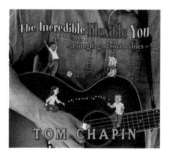

Egg Pass
- Collect an empty egg carton and eggs (plastic, shakers, or toy food) to fill carton.
- Cue music track 3: "The Plan."

Cooking Mix-Up
- Find a big empty bowl and a spoon.
- Consider having play food items or pictures of food at the ready in case your group needs more support.

Lesson Plan 2

Story Summary

Evan, Ellie, Jesse and Molly take a trip to the farm to visit Grandma and Grandpa and to make an apple pie and ice cream. They learn the difference between following their own plans versus the group plan. When they work together and follow a group plan, everyone feels good and they end up with a delicious treat to share.

The Lesson Flow

- Opening routine. (See page 42 in Introduction for more details.)
- Read the story, using the Teaching Moment suggestions included.
- Do Structured Activities.
- Reinforce the concept and vocabulary during the Dramatic Play activity.
- Closing routine. (See page 47 in Introduction for more details.)
- Send Family Letter home (Appendix C).

Teaching Moments - *The Group Plan*

Before you start to read the story, review concepts related to thoughts and feelings introduced in the previous lesson.

- Label the thought bubble (many times children think it is a cloud).
- Remind the group that it is the brain's job to make thoughts.
- Remind students about concepts related to feelings from Story 1. What emotions did we talk about (happy, sad, mad, scared)? How do we tell when someone is having a feeling and what it is? (We look at their face and their body for clues.) Prompt students to look at the initial illustration in this story and offer ideas on what they observe about the characters' facial expressions. For example, "Look at Ellie's face. How is she feeling? How can you tell?"

Guide children in making a smart guess about where the characters are going. Pose leading questions and point out the relevant details in the illustration (such as the barn and farm animals) that provide information about the content of the story.

- What do you see?
- What are the kids thinking about?
- Where are the kids going?

Introduce the new vocabulary concept in the story: "Today we are reading about Evan, Ellie, Jesse and Molly going to the farm. We will be learning about something we call the group plan."

Page 8

Point to the talking bubble and explain to the kids that Grandma is talking in this illustration. We can tell by the talking bubble coming out of her mouth. This is very different from a thinking bubble, which shows words we have in our heads. When we see talking bubbles it means words are coming out of the character's mouth.

Page 10

Look at what is happening in the illustration. Without Evan's help, they can't pick the apples. Jesse can't pick up the heavy ladder alone, Ellie can't reach the apples in the tree, and the only apple Molly can find has a worm in it.

Page 11

Notice the facial expressions of all the kids. How can we tell the kids are feeling happy? What clues do we see on their bodies and faces?

Page 14

Ask your students: "Who's not following the plan?" "Why does Evan feel upset?" Prompt students to look at the illustration and offer ideas on what they observe about the characters' facial expressions. Notice Jesse and Molly can carry the bucket together but Evan is feeling upset because it is too heavy to carry alone. When a member of the group follows his/her own plan, it can make others have upset feelings.

Page 15

Ask your students: "What did Ellie do that made Evan feel happy?" Prompt students to look at the illustration and offer ideas on what they observe about the characters' facial expressions. "Notice everyone is having fun because they are helping each other. Evan's feelings changed to happy when Ellie followed the plan."

Page 18

Prompt students to look at the illustration and offer ideas on what they observe about the characters' facial expressions. For example, "Look at Ellie's face. How is she feeling? How can you tell?"

Page 19

Ask your group what is different now that Jesse has changed his plan. "How is everyone feeling now? How can you tell?"

Page 22

Molly added silly ingredients to the bowl – they don't go into a pie! Ask your group questions that prompt them to look at the illustration and make a smart guess about how the characters are thinking and feeling. "What do you think Evan, Ellie and Jesse are thinking about Molly?" "How are the kids feeling?" "Do you think they like the smell of the mixture? How do we know? What clues do we see?"

Page 23

"Everyone is following the group plan! How is everyone feeling?"

Structured Activities

After you have completed the story and corresponding Teaching Moments, the following activities are used to reinforce the Social Thinking concept. Keep in mind that your purpose is to model the use of the vocabulary during teachable moments.

Draw attention to times when your students are following the group plan. It is important to use the vocabulary at the time you notice children doing the concepts well, so students can pay attention to what they are expected to do. If the vocabulary is used to tell children what not to do ("See Charlize, she isn't following the group plan."), then students pair the words with bad behavior and not as a tool through which they can learn positive lessons.

Use the book illustrations to provide a context for each of the activities. For example, when introducing the Apple Scramble game, show the corresponding illustration and remind your students how the children in the story followed the group plan to gather apples together.

Apple Scramble

In the story the children followed a group plan to gather apples for the pie. Now your students will follow a group plan to collect all of the scattered "apples" and put them back into a bucket.

1. Teacher places "apples" (balls of different sizes or paper cutouts of apples) into a bucket.
2. Teacher turns the bucket over to dump out the balls or scatters paper apples across the room.
3. Children follow a group plan to gather the apples and put them back into the bucket.

Use the vocabulary during Apple Scramble:
- "Our group plan is to put all of the apples in the bucket."
- "Calvin is thinking about the group plan and he is following the group plan."
- "Carter is playing with the blocks. Oops, he is not thinking about the group plan. He is following his own plan. That makes others feel frustrated."
- "Wow, Carter changed his plan! First he was building blocks but he saw the group was not doing this. Now he is collecting apples. He is thinking about others and following the group plan. The group feels good because Carter is helping! Carter feels good too!"

Milk Pail Obstacle Course

In the story, the children followed a group plan and worked together to carry heavy pails of milk back to Grandma. Now your students will work together to carry their pails through an obstacle course.

1. Set up materials for a simple obstacle course. Designate start and stop points.
2. Divide students into small groups of two or three.
3. Children work together to fill their pail with "milk" (paper balls, cotton balls, ping pong balls, etc.).
4. Children follow a group plan to carry their pail through the obstacle course.

Use the vocabulary during the Milk Pail Obstacle Course:
- "Our group plan is to carry the pails together."
- "Rylee and Blake are following the group plan. They are carrying the pail together."
- "Elena is carrying the pail by herself. Oops, she is not thinking about others. She is following her own plan."
- "Now Elena is carrying the pail with Stone! She is thinking about the group plan."

Activity 3 — Egg Pass

Let's look back at our story now and think about what happened next. The children needed to work together to gather eggs from the chicken coop. Now it's our turn to share a group plan. We're going to work together to fill this carton with eggs. Our group plan is to fill the carton with eggs.

1. Explain to your students: "The group plan is to pass eggs and fill the carton. When the music starts, pass the egg to the person sitting next to you. We will keep passing until the music stops. When the music stops, the person who is holding the egg will put it in the carton. Everyone will get a turn to put an egg in the carton!"
2. Teacher turns on the music and selects an egg from the chicken basket to pass.
3. Students pass the egg until the music stops. Student holding the egg places it in the carton. Repeat until every child has had a turn.
4. Provide examples of following your own plan so the students can see the contrast. For example, place an egg on your head (instead of following the group plan to pass the eggs) while the music plays.
5. When the carton is filled, reinforce the concept by stating, "We followed the group plan and filled a carton of eggs together!"
6. As you work to fill the egg carton, reinforce the concept that we all feel good when each person works as part of a group. Tell your students, "It makes me feel happy when I see everyone work together to follow the plan." Have your students take turns talking about how it feels when they follow the plan and see others working together.

Use the vocabulary during the Egg Pass game:
- "Sophie put an egg in the carton, she is following the group plan."
- "Miguel is passing an egg, he is following the group plan."
- "We are passing the egg as the music plays. Everyone is following the group plan."
- "Sammy - the music is playing but you are holding onto the egg! The group plan is to pass the egg."
- "When we work in a group, we think about each other and the group plan. Together we filled the carton with eggs!"

Activity 4 — Cooking Mix-Up

In the story the group plan was to find sugar for the apple pie. Molly followed her own plan and added lots of different foods into the bowl: olives, salad dressing, and pepper, YUCK! Now it is our turn to cook!

Let's see what our group makes* —will it be something delicious or something yucky? Our group plan is to cook together.

1. Get out an empty bowl and a spoon.
2. Explain to your students: "The group plan is to cook together. Everyone can add something to the bowl. Then we'll mix it all up and taste it."
3. Teacher pretends to put one ingredient into the bowl.
4. Each student takes a turn adding his or her own ingredient to the bowl.
5. When everyone has had a turn, it's time to stir the ingredients together. Tell your students: "Okay everybody, our group plan is to stir together. Everybody hold onto the spoon." Teacher holds onto the spoon. When everyone has their hand on the spoon, move hands together to pretend to stir.
6. Explain: "Now the group plan is to taste our food. Get your spoons out and take a bite."
7. Now pretend to eat the food. Teacher takes the first bite and with an exaggerated facial expression shows the group whether or not s/he liked it. Encourage students to do the same and watch others' faces to determine whether people like the food or not. This is great practice in reading others' nonverbal expressions and guessing what they are thinking.
8. Now "empty" the bowl and try making something new!

*If your group needs more structure or your students have difficulty with pretend play, consider using pictures of food items or even play food and having a specific item to make.

Use the vocabulary during the Cooking Mix-Up game:
● "Keisha added blueberries to the bowl. She is following the group plan."
● "Ishaan is stirring. He is following the group plan."
● "We are stirring together. Everyone is following the group plan."
● "Janine, the group plan is to *stir* right now. We'll taste it later."

Dramatic Play: Reinforcing the Concept and Vocabulary

Prepare Materials for Dramatic Play
- Gather images related to a farm to use as your children talk, brainstorm and plan.
- Copy template 2, Lesson 2 (Appendix A) that contains individual images of things found on a farm: a tractor, a chicken, eggs, a cow, a pig, and corn stalks. Cut out/enlarge images and have them handy to attach to your thought bubble prop.
- Located props to be used in recreating any of the ideas you or the children generate about a trip to the farm. Some props may overlap with previous activities. Some suggestions include:
  - Stuffed farm animals
  - Play dough, pie tin, or toy apple pie
  - Toy apples (can be reused from Structured Activity)
  - Cardboard box for barn, colored red
  - Feed bags
  - Garden items (toy rake, shovel, watering can) to plant and grow food
  - Toy tractors and trucks
  - Tools to fix tractors and trucks
  - Other farm related items

Going to the Farm
Using the Social Thinking concept and vocabulary during less structured playtime is a perfect opportunity to help children learn to use the vocabulary with their peers and appreciate the different aspects of following the group plan.

Set Up

"In our group we read the story about the children going to a farm. Today we are going to pretend to go to a farm. Let's think about a farm. What do we know?" (You can use the story to help provide context and/or items from the story found in Appendix A, Lesson 2, Template 2.)

- Who lives on a farm?
- What animals live on a farm?
- What kinds of buildings are on a farm?
- What do farmers do on their farm?
- What grows on a farm?
- What do farmers ride on?

As the children brainstorm, place pictures of items on your thought bubble (from Story 1). For example, if Edward shares that chickens live on the farm, place a picture of a chicken in the thought bubble. If a child shares an idea that is not part of the template, feel free to draw a quick sketch to visually represent it and attach it to the thought bubble.

"Together we thought about farms and all the different things we can see and do. Now let's make a group plan. What should we do on the farm together?"

Listen to your students brainstorm ideas for play. These might include:
- Make an apple pie (using play kitchen materials and play dough).
- Fix the broken tractor (play tools and vehicles).
- Pick apples from the trees.
- Pretend to plant and grow vegetables (using rakes, watering can, play seeds).
- Role play animals – pretend to be cows, chickens, horses.

Once the group has brainstormed ideas, it is time to play. You will go in one of the following directions with your group:
- Teacher chooses activities and everyone follows that plan.
- Take turns following each person's plan.
- Students put their ideas together to make a group plan.*

* Please remember, **some groups may not reach collaborative play for a long time!**

The goal of this dramatic play session is to illustrate the vocabulary in action. Model the use of the group plan in the context of the farm-related activities. Use the following examples as a guide to facilitating play.

Incorporate the thought bubble prop as you use the vocabulary. Tell your students, "The group plan is to pick apples. We are thinking about apples," as you place a picture of an apple in the thought bubble prop.

As play evolves, keep the thought bubble prop nearby. For example, if the group moves from picking apples to making pie, change the picture in the thought bubble from an apple to a pie.

"Jodie's plan is to push the wheelbarrow and Nancy's plan is to pick up apples. Let's make a group plan and put the apples in the wheelbarrow and push it together."

"Do you see what Maile and Rob are doing right now? What do you think their plan is?"

"Scott is cutting apples and Megan is rolling out the dough. Their plan is to make an apple pie."

"The group plan was to pick apples but we are almost done. Drew and Kristi are near the pigpen. Let's change the plan and feed apples to the pigs."

The final part of play is always clean up! Continue to use the vocabulary during this time. Examples include:

- "The group plan is to clean up!"
- "I'm thinking about putting away the apples."
- "Doug is thinking about cleaning up the animals."
- "We are all thinking about cleaning up together."

Beyond The Lesson: Generalize the Vocabulary to Other Settings

Just because the lesson is over doesn't mean the learning stops! Continue to use and reinforce the group plan vocabulary in future lessons and throughout your time together with students. Some suggestions follow.

While getting ready for group time:
- "It's circle time. The plan is to put your body in the group."
- "Laura is following the plan sitting in the circle."
- "The plan is to say 'hi' to everyone in the group."

Transitions:
- "Circle time is over. The plan is to go to the table for art. Let's all think of the group plan."
- "We are finished eating snack. Now the plan is to build with blocks."
- "The plan is to clean up toys now."

When group time is ending:
- "Today the group plan was to play farm."
- "Now our group is over. The plan is to go home."
- "The group plan is to get your backpack and wait by the door."

Take Away Points for This Lesson

On the following page you will find a list of the key core concepts we want students to take away from this lesson. Review the list and assess your student's knowledge based on the rubric below.

0 =	No understanding of the concept. They are not using the vocabulary or demonstrating any of the requisite associated behaviors.
1 =	Emerging awareness of the concept. May be able to point out or give examples of its use or misuse on others but are not demonstrating its use even with maximum support and cuing.
2 =	Emerging awareness of the concept. May be able to point out or give examples of its use or misuse on others and are demonstrating its use with support and cuing.
3 =	Solid understanding of the concept and can demonstrate its use with moderate cues.
4 =	Solid understanding of the concept and may be starting to use it with minimal cues.
5 =	Solid understanding of the concept and can demonstrate its use with minimal cues.

If you rate a student at 0 on the majority of the bullet points, consider:
The appropriateness of curriculum for this student. (See page 36 in introduction.)

If you rate a student at 1 or 2 on the majority of the bullet points, consider:
Spending more time teaching this concept before moving on to the next lesson. Explore it in different ways and across settings.

If you rate a student at 3 or above on the majority of the bullet points, consider:
Continuing to use the concept in context and teachable moments as you move forward in teaching the next lesson or deepening knowledge on this one.

Lesson ② Take Away Points for *The Group Plan*

The expectation is for kids to be exposed to (not master) the following concepts:

- Begin to understand that they are part of a group. When a teacher/parent uses words such as "everybody, class, friends, all, we, our, together" they are referring to a group, which includes each individual child.

- Begin to understand that a group has a plan.

- Build on information from Lesson 1 (everybody has his/her own thoughts). This lesson introduces the concept that we can think about something together.

- We refer to the books, games and activities we all do together as *the group plan*.

- Contrast the group plan with following your *own plan*.

- We do NOT expect kids to READ the group plan (i.e., look around and figure out what is going on) or necessarily to follow the plan. This teaching will come later. The aim in this lesson is to increase their awareness that there is an overall plan.

The Family Letter: Extending Learning Outside the Classroom

As children learn new Social Thinking vocabulary, it is helpful to solicit the help of parents and family members in using the same vocabulary at home.

Find the Family Letter in Appendix C and on the materials CD in the back of this book.

Lesson 2

The Group Plan

Family Letter and At Home Activities

In our Social Thinking group today we talked about the **group plan**. In our story, Evan, Ellie, Jesse and Molly take a trip to the farm to make an apple pie and ice cream. They learn the difference between following their *own plan* versus the *group plan*. When one person followed his/her own plan, the group could not accomplish their goal. When they worked together and followed the group plan everyone felt good and they ended up with delicious treats to share.

In our group we use illustrations to show everyone thinking about the group plan together versus a person who is thinking about his/her own plan. (See the illustration below.) We talk about "the plan" as a way to help children know what they are expected to think about and do when they are working in a group. When everyone is following the plan, we are all thinking about each other. When we all think about each other, everyone feels good.

Suggested ways to extend learning about the Group Plan at home:
- Talk about "the plan" and what you are thinking. For example, "My plan is to make a snack." "The plan is to go to the grocery store." "The plan is to get ready for bed! Time to brush our teeth; follow the plan."
- Talk about what each person can say and do so all share the same idea/plan. Consider the following examples: "I'm thinking of the plan to go to the grocery store. I'm getting my coat." "Sayida is thinking about the group plan. She is helping to set the table for dinner."
- Point out the times when you are all sharing one plan. Talk about how that makes you feel. For example, "We are following the plan to get ready to go to school. I put on my shoes. You put on your shoes too! That makes me feel happy. Now we're ready to go." Or use pictures and words.

Group plan/own plan illustration.

In the story, the group plan was to pick apples. Evan followed his own plan and pretended to drive a tractor.

Activity 1 At Home Activity: Following the Plan!
Anytime we do something together we are following a group plan. Reinforce the idea that children follow a plan when they are at home too, not just at school. At home a group plan might include cooking and eating dinner, folding laundry, raking leaves in the yard, going on a bicycle ride, or going to the grocery store. There is a connection between our behaviors and other people's emotions. When we follow a group plan, it makes other people feel happy and makes us feel good too!

Lesson 2. Template 1. Apples

Lesson 2. Template 2. Items Found on a Farm

Thinking With Your Eyes

Social Thinking Vocabulary
Thinking With Your Eyes

Definition
Receptively we use our eyes to gather information about what other people are thinking about, feeling, what is happening around us, and what might be someone else's plan.

Expressively we use our eyes to indicate our focus, which in turn cues others in on what we are thinking about; this could be an object, an event, or the people around us. **We also use our eyes expressively to show others we are thinking about them.**

Why Do We Teach this Concept?
One of the more common social "skills" we try to teach young children is to use their eyes for social referencing. Behavioral directives such as "look at me" are often used to encourage eye contact. As with all Social Thinking concepts, our aim is to teach the underlying thinking behind behavior. Therefore, the term *thinking with your eyes* will be used.

When children are taught to think with their eyes they begin to understand that there is a *purpose* for observing others and the environment. When you think with your eyes you are engaging in an active

process that helps you be aware of what is happening in your environment, determine what others are thinking and feeling, and subsequently know how to respond. It is more than just "looking" at something. Thinking is involved!

We can use what others are looking at to make a guess about what or whom they are thinking about.

Before Teaching the Lesson

- Read through the Lesson Plan and the Teaching Moment activities associated with it.
- Read through the storybook, noting the different places to Stop and Do, Stop and Notice, and/or Stop and Discuss.
- Read through the different Structured Activities to be done within the lesson.
- Prepare materials: create props, gather toys, print out images, etc. for the different activities.
- Familiarize yourself with the lyrics to the song used in teaching the lesson.
- Review the core concepts and rubric in the Take Away Points section of the lesson.
- Review the goal suggestions for this concept. (Find goals for all lessons in Appendix D.)

For example, if you are talking with a friend and he is looking at you this means he is thinking about you and what you are saying to him. If we are looking at something other than the person talking to us, like a picture on the wall, we are sending the message that we are thinking about the picture and not the person who is talking, since looking equals thinking.

The concept of thinking with your eyes is more complex than it sounds and needs to be taught in a series of sequential steps. These steps are integrated into the story and outlined below. Therefore, it is important to follow the recommended order of activities in this Lesson.

Eyes are like arrows, they point to what we are looking at.

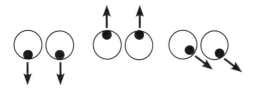

In the story, we see the alien's eyes looking at the rainbow backpack.

What we are looking at shows what we are thinking about. Looking equals thinking. For instance, in the story the alien is looking at the rainbow backpack. He is thinking about the backpack. We help students understand this concept by using arrows, something you can draw at any point to help your students too.

Once the connection between looking and thinking has begun, more advanced instruction can be added. You can now provide more information about what one can infer about another person's thoughts and what they might do next. For example, if the alien is looking at the backpack and thinking about it, it is likely that he may want to pick it up or see what's inside.

Prepare Materials for Structured Activities

What Am I Looking At?
- Fill backpack with at least six to eight items. Suggestions from the story include: map, pencil, cup, shirt, or shoes/boots. However, any common objects will work and you could use props from previous stories: blocks, stuffed animals, cars, etc. The important component is that each object should have a clear, identifiable function.
- Gather Wikki Stix® or pipe cleaners.

Astronaut Dress Up
- Gather costume supplies: one set per child
- Ideas include:
  - Helmet: bowl or colander
  - Moon boots: auto washing sponges attached to shoes by rubber bands
  - Jet pack: Glue two, two-liter bottles together. Cover with foil and tape together with electrical tape. Make straps out of electrical tape.

Music Activity
- Cue track 4 on the CD: "Think With Your Eyes."

Space Walk Activity
- Gather seating (chairs, beanbags, or carpet squares, one per child).
- Get your thought bubble prop.
- Find a steering wheel prop for your rocket ship (any round object will do).
- Decorate the room in an outer space theme.
- Enlarge and copy the illustrations of aliens (Appendix A). You will need one copy of each alien per child and one copy of each alien for the teacher.
- Enlarge and copy the illustration of planets (Appendix A). Only one copy of each planet is needed.
- Tape aliens and planets on walls around the room. Vary the location so they are placed in distinct spots, not too close to one another. Tape one alien per child next to a planet. For example, if you have three children in your group, tape three of the same alien next to the planet.

Lesson Plan ③

Story Summary

Evan, Ellie, Jesse and Molly take a trip in a rocket ship to outer space. They meet curious aliens. As the story unfolds, the aliens and children try to communicate but don't speak the same language. They have to learn to "think with their eyes" to figure out what the aliens are looking at, how that connects to what they are thinking about and therefore, what they are planning to do next.

The Lesson Flow

- Opening routine. (See page 42 in Introduction for more details.)
- Read the story, using the Teaching Moment suggestions included.
- Do Structured Activities.
- Reinforce the concept and vocabulary during the Dramatic Play activity.
- Closing routine. (See page 47 in Introduction for more details.)
- Send Family Letter home (Appendix C).

Teaching Moments – *Thinking With Your Eyes*

Before you read the story, review concepts introduced in the previous lessons.

Guide children in making a smart guess about where the characters are going. Pose leading questions and point out the relevant details in the illustration (such as the rocket ship and planets) that provide information about the content of the story.

- What do you see?
- What are the kids thinking about?
- Where are the kids going?

Introduce the new vocabulary concept in the story: "Today we are reading about Evan, Ellie, Jesse and Molly going into outer space. We will be learning about something we call thinking with your eyes."

Page 8
The kids get off the rocket ship and are looking at the alien planet. They do not see the aliens, but the aliens see the kids! Note: Some children might need to spend extra time learning about the word "alien" if it is not familiar. Show the illustration in the story and describe an alien as being a creature that lives in space.

Page 10

Notice the faint arrows in the illustration that connect the children's eyes to the space rocks. Trace the lines with your finger, so your students can clearly see the relationship between their eye gaze and the object.

Page 11

Trace the line between the characters' eyes and the space rocks. In addition, the thought bubble contains the space rocks to help emphasize they are looking at and thinking about the rocks.

Page 13

Although there are no arrows illustrated, trace the line between the alien's eyes and the backpack. In addition, the thought bubble contains the backpack to help emphasize the alien is looking at and thinking about the backpack.

Page 21

Have your students guess what the alien is looking at and thinking about before you turn the page.

Page 24

Ask your group, "What do you think the alien wants to do with the boots? What is his plan?"

Page 27

Take an opportunity to look at each alien. Have your students make a guess about which character each alien is looking at and thinking about.

Page 30

"How do we know the kids are thinking about each other? They are looking at each other."

Structured Activities

After you have completed the story and corresponding Teaching Moments, the following activities are used to reinforce the Social Thinking concept. Keep in mind that your purpose is to model the use of the vocabulary during teachable moments.

Draw attention to times when your students are thinking with their eyes. It is important to use the vocabulary at the time you notice children doing the concepts well, so students can pay attention to what they are expected to do. If the vocabulary is used to tell children what not to do ("See Brad, he's not thinking with his eyes."), then students pair the words with bad behavior and not as a tool through which they can learn positive lessons.

 ## What am I Looking At?

In the story, the children had to figure out what the alien wanted by thinking with their eyes. Now your students will have the opportunity to put this learning into action.

The goal of this activity is to assess how well your students can track your eye gaze and determine what you are looking at. Children will vary in their ability to do this. Some will understand the connection with relative ease, while it will take others a significant amount of time. Depending upon your students' abilities, your instruction may need to stay at this level until they are able to reliably identify what you are looking at.

- Take out the backpack and remove three items.
- Arrange items in a line in front of you, spread about six inches apart. There should be enough space in between to be able to visually make a clear distinction between objects.
- Tell your group, "Eyes are like arrows. They point to what someone is looking at."
- Look at each item individually and say, "I am looking at the _____." It can be helpful to use a pipe cleaner or wikki stix to make this connection more obvious. Make an arrow out of heavy construction paper and tape it to the end of the stick. Hold it near your eyes, pointing it in the direction of the item you are looking at. This makes your eye gaze easier to track.
- Change the items and take several new objects out of the backpack. It is now time to assess your student's ability to make the connection between your eye gaze and an object. Without using the arrow as a visual cue, look at one of the objects and ask a student, "What am I looking at?"
- Give each student an opportunity to take a turn so the more talkative kids don't give all the answers. Have your thought bubble handy. After they make the accurate guess, take the item, hold it up to your thought bubble and say, "*Yes*, I am looking at the _____, I am thinking about the _____."
- Mix up the order so the student doesn't just guess which object comes next in line.
- After you have gone through that cycle, next you will begin to establish a three-part connection: looking, thinking, and the plan. For example, "I am *looking* at the CUP and *thinking* about the CUP. What is my *plan*? What will I do with it?" (Take a drink!)
- Repeat the steps using the remaining items.

Thinking With Your Eyes High Fives

This is a quick activity to teach the concept that when we look at someone it shows we are thinking about that person.

- Look at a student and cue, "When I look at you, it means I'm thinking about you!" Then give each other a high five.
- Keeping your hand extended in the high five position, shift only your eyes to select another student. Cue if necessary, "When I look at you, it means I'm thinking about you and I'm ready for a high five!"
- Repeat steps so everyone in the group gets a turn. To make the activity less predictable, do not go in a specific order around the circle and give students multiple turns.
- If a student you are *not* looking at gives you a high five, verbalize where you are looking by giving the cue, "Oops! I am looking at Katie and thinking about Katie. I want to give Katie a high five now." While giving this cue, keep your eye gaze frozen on the student you are thinking about (Katie). For additional support, use your finger to trace a line through the air from your eye gaze to that student.
- Have students take a turn being the teacher. This is a great activity that demonstrates to our young learners the power of their eyes.

"Think With Your Eyes" Music Activity

This music activity teaches students that our eyes can send important information that helps us know what to do.

- Have all the children sit in a circle.
- Tell your students you are all going to play a follow the leader game. "When I look at you I am thinking about you and it will be your turn to be the leader. Everyone else needs to follow the leader's plan and do what the leader is doing with his or her hands."
- Next give suggestions and model the behavior. Have everyone practice (e.g. you could drum on the floor, tap your knees, clap your hands, tap your head).
- During the game, you will stop and pause the music. This will give you the opportunity to look at someone else and change the leader.
- Cue the CD to track 4, "Think With Your Eyes." (Find song lyrics in Appendix B.)

What am I Thinking About? Astronaut Dress Up

The Astronaut Dress Up game will reinforce the idea that what you are looking at shows what you are thinking about.

Tell your students: "We are going to pretend to be astronauts and we have to get dressed to go into space. Everyone will have a turn to choose what they want to wear. But you can't tell us with your words or show us with your hands. Just like the aliens in the book, we are going to think with our eyes to show others what we want!"

For the first turn, the teacher will model the activity.

- Make sure you have your thought bubble handy.
- As in the previous activity, line up several items in front of you (helmet bowls, space boot sponges, jet pack, etc.). Make sure there is enough distance (about six inches) in between the items.
- Next, "turn off" your voice. You can do this by pretending to zip your lips shut. Then, put your hands behind your back. Later, when your students take their turns, this will help them resist the temptation to gesture, point, or take the item.
- Tell your students you are thinking with your eyes and look at the first item you want to wear. For example, look at the space helmet and keep your eyes looking directly at it. Students then start guessing what you are looking at. Cue the group, "Think with your eyes. What am I looking at? What am I thinking about? What's my plan?"
- Once the group has guessed correctly, over exaggerate your feedback. For example, "You're right! I was looking at the space helmet, so I was thinking about the space helmet and my plan is to put the space helmet on my head!"
- Reinforce the connection between looking and thinking. Take the item (helmet) and place it clearly in your line of vision and then move it over to the thought bubble and then back to your line of vision and to the thought bubble again. This will help your students understand the concept more concretely.

 After you have modeled a turn, it is time for your students to try. Instead of calling out names, look at the students and cue, "When I look at you, it means I'm thinking about you. I will use my eyes to tell you it is your turn!" Give each student an opportunity to take a turn and put on astronaut gear.

What is My Plan? Space Walk

The goal of the space walk activity is for your students to think with their eyes to determine the plans of others. Before you begin, make sure your room is set up in a space theme. Please refer to the Prepare For Activities section for further details.

Arrange seating in a circle so students will be facing one another. This will be your pretend rocket ship for the activity. Tell your students, "Now our plan is to go on a space walk."

Follow the group plan and board the rocket ship together. Each child finds a place to sit.

Cue your students: "Remember, when we look at someone, it shows we are thinking about them. Now, show me you are thinking about me. If you are thinking about me, I can give you your space pack." When they do, say, "Nicky is looking at me. He is thinking about me." Give Nicky his space pack (brown paper bag) and then do the same with the rest of the students. The goal is for all students to understand they will receive their space pack by showing they are thinking about you with their eyes.

Share an imagination and pretend to blast off into space together. Instruct students to put down their space packs (to lessen the distraction), fasten their space seat belts and get ready to go. Have your students do a "countdown" and shake your chairs as you rocket up into the sky.

Once you are in outer space, remind the students you will be going on a space walk together. You will visit different planets and collect all of the aliens on that planet. Have students think with their eyes (look around the room) and discuss what they see. You might talk about the planets and aliens posted around the room.

For the first turn, the teacher will model the activity. (Have your thought bubble prop nearby.)

- Use a prop steering wheel to signify you are the pilot of the rocket ship. As the pilot, you get to make the plan and choose where to fly the rocket.
- Look around the room and say, "I have a plan. Now I have to show you what I'm thinking about." Choose an alien and planet posted on the wall and look at it.
- Encourage students to think with their eyes to determine which planet you are looking at and thinking about. Maintain your eye gaze on the planet while you talk.
- Once a correct guess has been made, place a copy of the alien you were looking at in your thought bubble prop. Verbal cue: "That's right! I'm looking at the green planet and alien. My plan is to get that green alien!" The key here is to emphasize the connection between looking, thinking, and the plan (what you intend to do).
- Pretend to fly the rocket to the planet. Only the pilot gets out to collect all the aliens.

Once you are back in the rocket, tell the group, "I will give you an alien when you are thinking about me with your eyes." Distribute accordingly as children are looking at you. Have children place the aliens in their space packs to lessen distraction.

Take turns letting each student be the rocket ship pilot. It will always be the plan of the pilot to determine which planet to visit, think with his/her eyes so the others know where the pilot intends to go, get out of the rocket, collect the aliens, and bring them inside. The pilot can then pass out the aliens to peers – but only to those who are thinking about him/her with their eyes.

The game is over when everyone has had a turn or all aliens have been collected. Return to earth and exit the rocket.

Dramatic Play: Reinforcing the Concept and Vocabulary

Prepare Materials for Dramatic Play

- Gather images related to a trip to outer space to use as your children talk, brainstorm and plan.
- Copy template 1, Lesson 3 (Appendix A) that contains individual images of things found in outer space: a meteor, stars, comets, and a rocket ship. Cut out/enlarge images and have them handy to attach to your thought bubble prop.
- Locate props to be used in recreating any of the ideas you or the children generate about a trip to outer space. Some props may overlap with previous activities. Some suggestions include:
  - Flashlights
  - Glow in the dark stars and planets
  - Space rocks (painted rocks)
  - Telescopes (paper towel tubes)
  - Globe
  - Photos of rocket ships
  - Backpacks
  - Control panel for rocket ship (board with knobs glued on)

A Trip to Outer Space

Using the Social Thinking concept and vocabulary during less structured playtime is a perfect opportunity to help children learn to use the vocabulary with their peers and appreciate that thinking with your eyes is an important aspect of being around others.

Set Up

Begin by telling students, "In our group we read the story about going to outer space. Today we are going to pretend to make a trip ourselves. Let's think about space. What do we know?"

You can use the story to help provide context and items from space that you've copied and cut out for previous activities (using templates in Appendix A). Consider the following to help your group think about outer space:

- Who goes to outer space?
- How do we get to outer space?
- What can we find in outer space?
- Who lives in outer space?
- Where can we go in outer space?
- What can we do in outer space?

As the children brainstorm, place pictures of items in your thought bubble. For example, if Ashley shares that we ride in a rocket ship to go to outer space, place the picture of the rocket in the thought bubble. If a child shares an idea not represented by one of the images, feel free to draw a quick sketch and place it in the thought bubble.

Verbally cue students: "Together we thought about outer space and all the different things we can see and do. Now let's make a group plan. What should we do in outer space together?"

Listen to your students brainstorm ideas for play. Suggestions may include:
- Act out the story.
- Build a rocket and blast off.
- Land on different planets and explore.
- Role play - pretend to be astronauts and aliens. Wear the costumes from the earlier dress up activity.
- Fly the rocket through space, avoiding obstacles like meteor showers.
- Fix the rocket when parts fall off or break down.
- Play the Space Walk game above with less structure.

Once the group has brainstormed ideas, it is time to decide on a group play plan. You will go in one of the following directions with your students:
- Teacher chooses activities and everyone follows that plan.
- Take turns following each child's plan.
- Students put their ideas together to make a group plan.*

* Please remember, **some groups may not reach collaborative play for a long time!**

The goal of dramatic play is to illustrate the vocabulary in action. Model the use of thinking with your eyes in the context of going to outer space and related activities. Use the following examples as a guide to facilitating play:
- Use the thought bubble prop as you use the vocabulary to comment and draw attention to times when you are thinking with your eyes. Take materials from play and hold them up to your eyes and then the thought bubble and then back to your eyes and the thought bubble again.
- Do the same to point out times when children are thinking with their eyes.
  - "Kathi is thinking with her eyes. She is looking at the steering wheel and thinking about being the pilot of the rocket ship." (Hold the steering wheel in her line of vision, then up to the thought bubble and repeat.)
  - "Marty is thinking about the group plan to fix the broken rocket ship. He is looking around for tools. Maybe you can think with your eyes and help him find tools and work on the ship together?"
  - "Think with your eyes. I wonder what Kate is pretending to fix on that rocket ship."

- Help kids practice thinking with their eyes to determine what a person might do next.
  - "Ron is thinking with his eyes about the hammer. His plan is to fix the broken part on our rocket."
  - "Cheryl is thinking with her eyes about the purple planet. What is her plan?"

The final part of the play is always clean up! Continue to use the vocabulary during this time. Examples include:

- "Think with your eyes – what do we need to clean up?"
- "Think with your eyes – have we put all the toys away?"
- "I'm thinking about something that needs to be picked up! Think with your eyes to figure out what it is."

Beyond the Lesson: Generalize the Vocabulary to Other Settings

Just because the lesson is over doesn't mean the learning stops! Continue to use and reinforce the vocabulary in future lessons and throughout your time together with students. Some suggestions follow.

While getting ready for group time:
- "Think with your eyes – kids are sitting down, it must be time to start our group."
- "Think with your eyes and show me what color carpet square you want to sit on."
- "You will know it is your turn when I am looking at you and thinking about you."
- "I'm looking at and thinking about Lily. That means it's Lily's turn to pick a carpet square."

Transitions:
- "When I'm thinking with my eyes about you, it is your turn to line up to go to art."
- "We are done with circle time. What is next? I'm thinking about it with my eyes."
- "It's snack time. Ariel is my snack helper today. Think about her with your eyes to show you are ready for your crackers."

When group time is ending:
- "When I think with my eyes about you, you can stand up and get your backpack."
- "Line up at the door when I think about you with my eyes."
- "Who am I thinking about now? That's right, I'm thinking about Pam. It's Pam's turn to line up."
- "Are you saying goodbye to me or the floor? Your eyes are looking at the floor. Show me you are thinking about me! Now your eyes are looking at me, you are thinking about me. Bye!"

Take Away Points for This Lesson

On the following page you will find a list of the key core concepts we want students to take away from this lesson. Review the list and assess your student's knowledge based on the rubric below.

0 =	No understanding of the concept. They are not using the vocabulary or demonstrating any of the requisite associated behaviors.
1 =	Emerging awareness of the concept. May be able to point out or give examples of its use or misuse on others but are not demonstrating its use even with maximum support and cuing.
2 =	Emerging awareness of the concept. May be able to point out or give examples of its use or misuse on others and are demonstrating its use with support and cuing.
3 =	Solid understanding of the concept and can demonstrate its use with moderate cues.
4 =	Solid understanding of the concept and may be starting to use it with minimal cues.
5 =	Solid understanding of the concept and can demonstrate its use with minimal cues.

If you rate a student at 0 on the majority of the bullet points, consider:
The appropriateness of curriculum for this student. (See page 36 in introduction.)

If you rate a student at 1 or 2 on the majority of the bullet points, consider:
Spending more time teaching this concept before moving on to the next lesson. Explore it in different ways and across settings.

If you rate a student at 3 or above on the majority of the bullet points, consider:
Continuing to use the concept in context and teachable moments as you move forward in teaching the next lesson or deepening knowledge on this one.

Lesson **3** Take Away Points for *Thinking With Your Eyes*

The expectation is for kids to be exposed to (not master) the following concepts:

- Begin to understand that there is a *purpose* for observing others and the environment.

- We use our eyes to gather information about what is happening around us, the group plan, and what other people are thinking and feeling.

- We also use our eyes to show others we are thinking about them.

- Eyes are like arrows, they point to what someone is looking at.

- Begin to understand the connection between looking and thinking. When people are looking at something or someone, they are thinking about that object or person. This helps us figure out their plan or what they might do next.

The Family Letter: Extending Learning Outside the Classroom

As children learn new Social Thinking vocabulary, it is helpful to solicit the help of parents and family members in using the same vocabulary at home.

Find the Family Letter in Appendix C and on the materials CD in the back of this book.

Lesson 3

Thinking With Your Eyes

Family Letter and At Home Activities

In our Social Thinking group today we talked about **thinking with your eyes.** Expressively we use our eyes to show others what we are thinking about. We look at people to let them know we are thinking about *them*, listening to *them*, talking to *them*, and/or sharing an experience with *them*. Receptively we use our eyes to gather information about what other people are thinking about, what is happening around us and what might be someone else's plan.

In the story we read, Evan, Ellie, Jesse and Molly take a trip in a rocket ship to outer space. They meet curious aliens. As the story unfolds, the aliens and children try to communicate but don't speak the same language. The children have to learn to think with their eyes to figure out what the aliens are looking at, how that connects to what they are thinking about and therefore, what they are planning to do next.

We will be using the term thinking with your eyes instead of behavioral directives such as "look at me" or "use eye contact." When children are taught to think with their eyes they begin to understand that there is a purpose for observing others and the environment. When you think with your eyes you are engaging in an active process that helps you determine what others are thinking, how they are feeling, and subsequently how to respond. It is more than just "looking" at something. Thinking is involved!

What a person is looking at is often what he or she is thinking about. We can use what others are looking at to make a smart guess about what or whom they are thinking about. For example, if you are talking with a friend and he is looking at you this means he is thinking about you and what you are saying to him. If we are looking at something other than the person talking to us, like a picture on the wall, we are sending the message that we are thinking about the picture and not the person who is talking, since looking equals thinking.

Eyes are like arrows, they point to what someone is looking at and most likely thinking about!

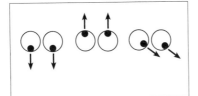

Lesson 3. Template 1. Items Found in Outer Space

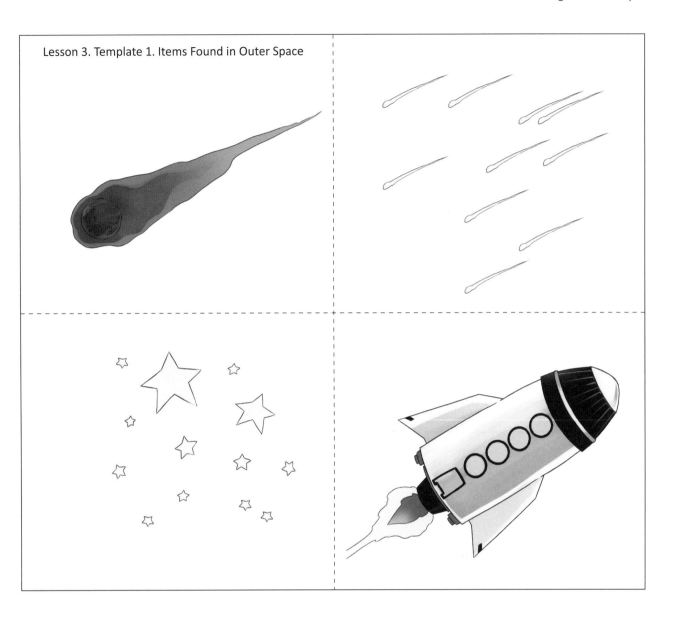

Lesson 3. Template 2. Aliens

Lesson 3. Template 3. Planets

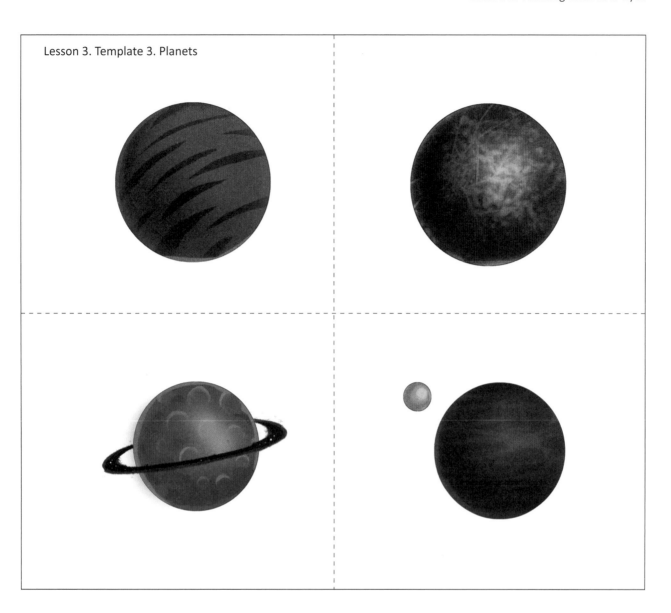

Body in the Group

Social Thinking Concept Targeted
Body in the Group

Definition
Keeping your *body in the group* means maintaining a comfortable physical presence around others – not too close, yet not too far away. When your body is in the group, it sends the nonverbal message that you are interested in others and that you are following the same plan. The opposite is also true. If your body is out of the group – it is too far away – it sends the message you are not thinking about the group.

Why Do We Teach this Concept?
While we often realize the importance of verbal language and what to say in a conversation, it is important to understand that physical proximity is also a key ingredient to successful social interactions. When we share space with others, we show we are engaged and interested in the group through our physical presence.

Before Teaching the Lesson

- Read through the Lesson Plan and the Teaching Moment activities associated with it.
- Read through the storybook, noting the different places to Stop and Do, Stop and Notice, and/or Stop and Discuss.
- Read through the different Structured Activities to be done within the lesson.
- Prepare materials: create props, gather toys, print out images, etc. for the different activities.
- Familiarize yourself with the lyrics to the song used in teaching the lesson.
- Review the core concepts and rubric in the Take Away Points section of the lesson.
- Review the goal suggestions for this concept. (Find goals for all lessons in Appendix D.)

Prepare Materials for Stop and Do Activities

Page 7. Stop and Do Activity
- Make copies of sea creatures from story (Appendix A).
- Place sea creatures in a bag.

Prepare Materials for Structured Activities

Freeze and Group Swim
- Music player
- Cue track 5 on the CD: "Body in the Group."

Islands Game
- Create three islands around your room. You can use any material that designates a clear and defined space. Examples include: using blankets, carpet squares, or painters tape (in the shape of an island) on the floor.
- Gather materials to make three distinct island themes. Examples may include:
  - Stuffed animals for an animal island
  - Blocks and tools for a building island
  - Play food for a cooking island
  - Bubbles for a bubble island
- Arrange materials on each island.

Obstacle Course
- Select two to three obstacles per course to start. Add more as your students become more familiar with the concept and gain a greater awareness of keeping their bodies in the group.
- Set up obstacles to reflect the scenes from the story.
  - Coral Reef: foam blocks, carpet squares, bean bags; attach paper fish or toy fish to the materials.
  - Seaweed Jungle: hang green paper streamers in the doorway or around a small table. You might also put them in a large pile on the floor.
  - Sunken Ship: hang a sheet over a small table or use a cardboard box.
  - Sea Cave: a fabric tunnel.

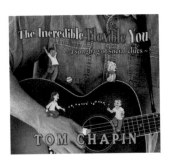

Lesson Plan 4

Story Summary

In this story, Evan, Ellie, Jesse and Molly take a trip to the ocean. The group plan is to find a shark tooth and they quickly realize they need to think about each other and keep their bodies in a group to find it. When they keep their bodies in the group they finally find the shark tooth … and something they weren't expecting!

The Lesson Flow

- Opening routine. (See page 42 in Introduction for more details.)
- Read the story, using the Teaching Moment suggestions included.
- Do Structured Activities.
- Reinforce the concept and vocabulary during the Dramatic Play activity.
- Closing routine. (See page 47 in Introduction for more details.)
- Send Family Letter home (Appendix C).

Teaching Moments - *Body in the Group*

Before you read the story, review concepts introduced in the previous lessons.

Guide children in making a smart guess about where the characters are going. Pose leading questions and point out the relevant details in the opening illustration that provide information about the content of the story.

- What do you see?
- What are the kids thinking about?
- Where are the kids going?

Introduce the new vocabulary concept in the story: "Today we are reading about Evan, Ellie, Jesse and Molly going on an underwater adventure. We will be learning about something we call body in the group."

Page 7

There are many octopuses but their bodies are not together. They are not a group. Can you find other groups? What else can you find?

Mention to students that groups can be large and small and that even two animals together can be a group.

Make copies of the sea creature illustrations (find these in Appendix A and on the materials CD). Place images in a bag. Have each child reach in and choose an animal. Take turns putting each sea creature in the middle of the circle so they form a group. The purpose of this Stop and Do activity is for the children to physically manipulate the animals to see them move in and out of the group.

Page 9

When the kids are too close together, they are feeling uncomfortable and upset. Highlight the facial expressions on the children.

Page 10

Notice how the kids' facial expressions and feelings change once they are a good distance apart. They feel better when they have room to move.

Page 11

Notice how the characters feel uncomfortable because they are too far away from each other.

Page 12

In life, we experience many different types of groups in all the places we go. In this illustration, point out the small group of fish. They are in a group at school!

Page 14

This illustration provides an opportunity to discuss yet another kind of group – one based on a shared activity. Notice the crabs. Two crabs are in a music group playing instruments together. One crab, the one playing the horn, has his body out of the group.

Page 16

Here we see an example of another group: a family group! Look at the sea turtles together on the blanket sharing some seaweed.

Page 23

Make a smart guess with your group. What do the characters see?

Structured Activities

After you have completed the story and corresponding Teaching Moments, the following activities are used to reinforce the Social Thinking concept. Keep in mind that your purpose is to model the use of the vocabulary during teachable moments.

Draw attention to times when your students have their bodies in the group. It is important to use the vocabulary at the time you notice children doing the concepts well, so students can pay attention to what they are expected to do. If the vocabulary is used to tell children what not to do ("See Beryl, she doesn't have her body in the group"), then students pair the words with bad behavior and not as a tool through which they can learn positive lessons.

Activity
1

"In the Group" Music Activity

The purpose of this activity is to raise your students' awareness of their physical proximity in a group. We put our bodies in a group so we can be part of the plan. Often we need to directly instruct what an expected distance is and have students practice what it looks like to be in or out of a group.

Using the illustrations as a guide, review pages 9 and 11 in the story. Evan, Ellie, Jesse and Molly learned to keep their bodies in the group – not too close yet not too far away. Now your students will have the opportunity to practice this concept as well.

- Instruct your group to stand up in a circle.
- While standing, have each child hold one arm out to the side.
- If a child's arm touches another child, the child is standing too close. If the child is more than one arm's length away, the child is too far away.
- Cue track 5 on the CD: "In the Group."
- Tell them the plan is to put some music on and have a dance party. When the music stops, it is time to FREEZE. Freezing means to stop moving every part of your body.
- Start the music and encourage children to dance around the room.
- Pause the song briefly throughout and children FREEZE. Encourage them to think with their eyes to look around the room. Then, discuss the physical presence of everyone. Is it still a group or are there kids all over the room? Whose body is still in the group? Who danced out? The objective of the activity is to observe and discuss what happened during the dancing fun.
- It may be helpful to photograph or video tape your group during this activity and then review. It is often easier for children to look at still images to see what they look like when their bodies are in or out of the group.

Activity
2

Islands

The purpose of this activity is to explore what it means to have your body in the group as one sits, stands, and moves. Because having your body in a group can look different depending upon the context, it is important to practice this concept in a variety of settings and activities. It is easier to keep your body in the group when the space is well defined, such as sitting at a table, than when up and moving. Therefore, we also have to practice putting our bodies in a group when standing and walking in a line.

- Set up three distinct islands with coordinating materials as described in the preparation section of this lesson.
- Tell your group you will be exploring the islands together. Each island has something fun to find and do.
- Explain that the children must keep their bodies in the group to travel to the island. Move from island to island in the following ways:
  ○ Pretend to swim together to get to the island. Use the vocabulary as you move. For example, "Everyone has their body in the group! Not too close, not too far. We are swimming together in a group."
  ○ Stand in a line and walk together to the island. Again, use the vocabulary as you move. "I'm thinking with my eyes and I see that everyone has his or her body in the line. This looks like a group!"
  ○ Send each student one by one to the island. This provides a contrast to demonstrate what it looks like to have your body out of the group. For example, "Kennedy's body is out of the group. She is walking to the next island by herself."
- Upon arrival at an island, give the group time to explore and play with the materials. While on an island, it is important to keep your body in the group. Remind your students that when their body is in the group, it lets everyone know they are thinking about others and interested in playing. Have fun with the idea that you are pretending to play on the island. If your body goes out of the group, you will fall into the water!

 Activity 3 Obstacle Course

The obstacle course activity provides another way to practice keeping your body in the group while the group is in motion.

Set up an obstacle course that mimics scenes from the story. It is recommended to start small and only arrange two to three obstacles at first. Try this activity a few times and add extra obstacles as your students become more familiar with it and gain a greater awareness of keeping their body in the group.

- Coral reef
- Sunken ship
- Seaweed jungle
- Sea cave

Instruct students to put their bodies in the group. Explain that you will be doing an obstacle course together. The goal is to do it as a group and find a shark tooth (or shark).

It can be challenging for kids to keep their body in the group while waiting for a turn in the obstacle course! It may be helpful to physically define a "waiting area" so children have a more concrete visual of where to stand and wait. Setting up chairs or standing in a hula-hoop can be helpful.

Demonstrate how to complete each obstacle.

Instruct one child to go through the first activity in the obstacle course. The remaining children must keep their bodies in the group while waiting for their turn.

After every child has had an opportunity to go through the first obstacle, mention that when everyone's body is back in the group you will move on to the next activity in the obstacle course. Pretend to swim to the next obstacle together.

Continue through the remaining obstacles in the same manner.

Optional: At the end of the last obstacle, have a shark puppet, toy, or a picture of the shark from the book waiting. Go back through the course in reverse order to escape from the shark. Once you are "safe" again, discuss how students kept their bodies in the group (or did not!) as you all swam away quickly.

Dramatic Play: Reinforcing the Concept and Vocabulary

Prepare Materials for Dramatic Play

- Gather images related to an adventure in the ocean to use as your children talk, brainstorm and plan.
- Copy template 1, Lesson 4 (Appendix A) that contains individual images of things found in the ocean: a boat, fish, crabs, turtles, octopuses, and a sunken ship. Cut out/enlarge images and have them handy to attach to your thought bubble prop.
- Locate props to be used in recreating any of the ideas you or the children generate about the underwater adventure. Some props may overlap with previous activities. Some suggestions for scuba gear include:
  - Goggles or sunglasses
  - Flexible straw
  - Flippers
  - Scuba tanks (clear liter bottles, aquarium tubing or straw)
- Find materials to build a boat (blocks, cardboard box).
- Find materials that relate to being on the beach, such as shells, towels, sand toys, etc.

A Trip to the Ocean

Using the Social Thinking concept and vocabulary during less structured playtime is a perfect opportunity to help children learn to use the vocabulary with their peers and appreciate that getting one's body in the group is an important aspect of being around others.

Set Up

Begin by telling students, "In our group we read the story about going to the ocean. Today we are going to pretend to take a trip ourselves. Let's think about the ocean. What do we know?" You can use the story to help provide context and items from the story on template 1 in Appendix A and on the materials CD. Consider the following to help your group think about the ocean:

- How can we get to the ocean?
- What could we wear to the ocean?
- Who lives in the ocean?
- What do different animals do in the ocean?
- What can we do in the ocean?

As the children brainstorm, place pictures of items in your thought bubble. For example, if Charlotte shares that we can travel by boat to the ocean, place the picture of the boat in the thought bubble. If a child shares an idea that is not pictured, feel free to draw a quick sketch to visually represent the idea.

Verbally cue students: "Together we thought about the ocean and all the different things we can see and do. Now let's make a group plan. What should we do at the ocean?"

Listen to your students brainstorm ideas for play. Suggestions for ideas might include:
- Keep the obstacles set up from the above activity.
- Fly a water plane and land in the ocean.
- Put on scuba gear and take a swim.
- Build a boat and row out to sea.
- Role play - pretend to be different sea animals. Move like an octopus or jump like a dolphin.

Once the group has brainstormed ideas, it is time to make a play plan. You will go in one of the following directions with your group:
- Teacher chooses activities and everyone follows that plan.
- Take turns following each child's plan.
- Students put their ideas together to make a group plan.*

* Please remember, **some groups may not reach collaborative play for a long time!**

The goal of play is to illustrate the vocabulary in action. Model the use of body in the group in the context of activities related to the ocean. Use the following examples as a guide to facilitating play.

Use the thought bubble prop as you use the vocabulary to provide visual feedback to students. Take materials from play and hold them up to your eyes and then to the thought bubble and then back to your eyes and the thought bubble again.

"Beatrice has her body in the group. She is thinking about playing with the group."

"Mei and Kellen have their bodies in the group getting dressed in the scuba gear. Maybe Lea can put her body in the group and bring the goggles over."

"Heather is putting on her goggles and Krista is wearing flippers. I wonder what Laurie will wear when she puts her body in the group?"

"Laura, Megan, and Erikka have their bodies in the group exploring the sea cave together."

"Katie looks afraid of the shark. Maybe we could pretend he is a friendly shark. Let's put our bodies in the group and have a tea party together."

The final part of play is always clean up! Continue to use the vocabulary during this time. Examples include:
- "Put your bodies in the group and clean up the scuba gear."
- "Billy and Matt have their bodies in the group. They are cleaning up the sea cave."
- "When all the toys are cleaned up, put your body in the group for circle time."

Beyond The Lesson: Generalize the Vocabulary to Other Settings

Just because the lesson is over doesn't mean the learning stops! Continue to use and reinforce the vocabulary in future lessons and throughout your time together with students. Some suggestions follow.

While getting ready for group time:
- "Put your body in the group and sit down for circle time."
- "I will know we are ready to start when I see everyone's body in the group."
- "Hang up your backpack and put your body in the group."

Transitions:
- "Put your body in the group so we can eat our snack."
- "When your body is out of the group, it looks like you are not ready to play our next game."

When group time is ending:
- "Put your body in the group by the door."
- "Put your body in the group with mom. This shows her you are ready to go home."
- "Keep your body in the group when you walk to the car."

Take Away Points for This Lesson

On the following page you will find a list of the key core concepts we want students to take away from this lesson. Review the list and assess your student's knowledge based on the rubric below.

0 =	No understanding of the concept. They are not using the vocabulary or demonstrating any of the requisite associated behaviors.
1 =	Emerging awareness of the concept. May be able to point out or give examples of its use or misuse on others but are not demonstrating its use even with maximum support and cuing.
2 =	Emerging awareness of the concept. May be able to point out or give examples of its use or misuse on others and are demonstrating its use with support and cuing.
3 =	Solid understanding of the concept and can demonstrate its use with moderate cues.
4 =	Solid understanding of the concept and may be starting to use it with minimal cues.
5 =	Solid understanding of the concept and can demonstrate its use with minimal cues.

If you rate a student at 0 on the majority of the bullet points, consider:
The appropriateness of curriculum for this student. (See page 36 in introduction.)

If you rate a student at 1 or 2 on the majority of the bullet points, consider:
Spending more time teaching this concept before moving on to the next lesson. Explore it in different ways and across settings.

If you rate a student at 3 or above on the majority of the bullet points, consider:
Continuing to use the concept in context and teachable moments as you move forward in teaching the next lesson or deepening knowledge on this one.

Lesson 4 Take Away Points for *Body in the Group*

The expectation is for kids to be exposed to (not master) the following concepts:

- Keeping your body in the group means maintaining a comfortable physical presence around others – not too close, yet not too far away.

- When your body is in the group, it sends the nonverbal message that you are interested in others and that you are following the same plan. This makes others feel comfortable about sharing space with you. The opposite is also true. When your body is not in the group, it sends the nonverbal message that you are not interested in others, which can make others feel uncomfortable about sharing space with you.

- Having your body in a group can look different depending upon the situation (the context): sitting at a table, standing/walking in a line, sitting in a circle on the floor.

- A group is when two or more people are together sharing space and a plan.

The Family Letter: Extend Learning Outside the Classroom

As children learn new Social Thinking vocabulary, it is helpful to solicit the help of parents and family members in using the same vocabulary at home.

Find the Family Letter in Appendix C and on the materials CD in the back of this book.

Lesson 4

Body in the Group

Family Letter and At Home Activities

In the *Body in the Group* story, Evan, Ellie, Jesse and Molly take a trip to the ocean. The group plan is to find a shark tooth and they quickly realize they need to think about each other and keep their bodies in a group to find it. When they keep their bodies in the group they finally find the shark tooth … and something they weren't expecting!

In our social thinking group we learned about the concept of **body in the group**. Keeping your body in the group means maintaining a comfortable physical presence around others – not too close, yet not too far away. When your body is in the group, it sends the nonverbal message that you are interested in others and that you are following the same plan. The opposite is also true. If your body is out of the group (too far away), it sends the message you are not thinking about the group. While we often realize the importance of language and what to say in a conversation, it is important to understand that physical proximity is also a key ingredient to successful social interactions.

Body in the group.

Body out of the group.

Activities to try at home

Activity 1 Use the body in the group vocabulary throughout your daily routines. Keep in mind that any time two people are sharing space, they are considered a group. Therefore, you can use the vocabulary when you and your child are alone, or when the family is together as a whole. Consider the following examples:

- "We can start our movie when all family members have their bodies in the group."
- "It's time for dinner. Everyone in the family has their body in the group, sitting at the table. We can start our meal together!"
- "When you leave the table, your body is out of the group. It makes me think you are finished with your meal."
- "Remember to keep your body in the group when we shop together at the grocery store."

Lesson 4. Template 1. Items found in the Ocean

Lesson 4. Template 2. Items found in the Ocean

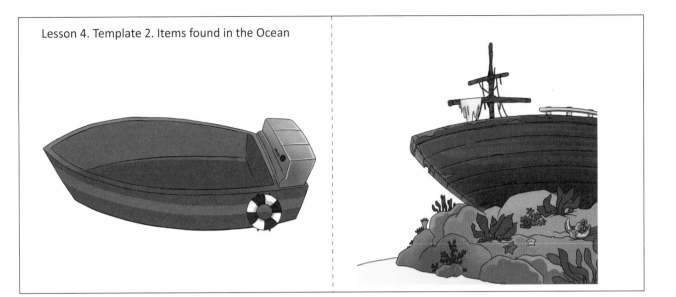

Whole Body Listening

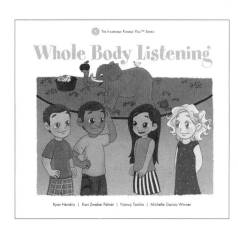

Social Thinking Concept Targeted
Whole Body Listening*

Definition
Whole body listening is when your eyes, ears, mouth, hands, arms, legs and feet are calm and quiet. When your body is calm and quiet you are able to listen with your *whole* body; it helps you pay attention to what people are doing around you and it shows others you are thinking about them.

Why Do We Teach this Concept?
Listening is an active process that helps students organize their bodies and minds to help them be more available to fully process what is happening around them. It involves demonstrating to others that we are thinking about what they are doing and saying. It also means that we are thinking about them as we consider their words and feelings in the context of the situation. It involves looking like we are interested in what is going on, even when we may be somewhat bored by the subject matter.

We introduce the child-friendly vocabulary whole body listening so our students begin to understand that listening is more than just using their ears. Exploring this concept helps increase our students' awareness of both how we listen and the nonverbal messages we are

sending when we are part of a group and when others are talking with and to us. Listening with our whole bodies, and subsequently focusing on and thinking about the group, sets the stage for successful communication and interaction.

Before Teaching the Lesson

- Read through the Lesson Plan and the Teaching Moment activities associated with it.
- Read through the storybook, noting the different places to Stop and Do, Stop and Notice, and/or Stop and Discuss.
- Read through the different Structured Activities to be done within the lesson.
- Prepare materials: create props, gather toys, print out images, etc. for the different activities.
- Familiarize yourself with the lyrics to the song used in teaching the lesson.
- Review the core concepts and rubric in the Take Away Points section of the lesson.
- Review the goal suggestions for this concept. (Find goals for all lessons in Appendix D.)

---

* Whole body listening is a concept created in 1990 by Susanne Poulette Truesdale and first described in her article, "Whole-Body Listening: Developing Active Auditory Skills" (Language Speech and Hearing Services in School, Vol. 21, 1090, 183-184). Read the article via Eric (www.eric.ed.gov) or at the American Speech and Hearing Association (ASHA) website: www.asha.org.

Prepare Materials For Structured Activities

"Listen With All Of You" Music Activity

- Prep music player to track 6.
- Preview lyrics (Appendix B).

Zoo Adventure/Acting Out the Story

Turn your room into a pretend zoo!

- Designate and decorate specific areas of the room for all the animals in the story: alligators, flamingos, chameleons, monkeys, cheetahs, lion, elephants, giraffes. You can photocopy pictures of animals from the story or use stuffed animals for props.
- Make a giraffe puppet out of a brown paper bag.
- Make leaves out of construction paper to feed the giraffe.

Lesson Plan 5

Story Summary

Evan, Ellie, Jesse and Molly take a trip to the zoo. They learn that when all of their body parts are calm and quiet, it shows others they are thinking about them. When they listen with their whole bodies, they get to visit and learn about lots of animals, and everyone feels good about being together.

The Lesson Flow

- Opening routine. (See page 42 in Introduction for more details.)
- Read the story, using the Teaching Moment suggestions included.
- Do Structured Activities.
- Reinforce the concept and vocabulary during the Dramatic Play activity.
- Closing routine. (See page 47 in Introduction for more details.)
- Send Family Letter home (Appendix C).

Teaching Moments – *Whole Body Listening*

Before you read the story, review concepts introduced in the previous lessons.

Guide children in making a smart guess about where the characters are going. Pose leading questions and point out the relevant details in the illustration (such as the zoo animals) that provide information about the content of the story.

- What do you see?
- What are the kids thinking about?
- Where are the kids going?

Introduce the new vocabulary concept in the story: "Today we are reading about Evan, Ellie, Jesse and Molly going to the zoo. We will be learning about something we call whole body listening."

Stop and Notice

Page 8

Take a moment to connect what is happening in the story with the real life setting of your classroom. Are your students listening with their whole bodies? Offer up positive feedback that draws attention to what is expected. For example, "I see Rubi has listening hands and feet and Brenda is listening with her mouth. Carlos is making his whole body listen."

Page 9

The kids know where to go because they were listening with their whole bodies.

Page 10

In the illustration, Evan's words are being "interrupted" by the actions of the other kids. Although the others are not talking at the same time (how we typically think of interrupting) the big movements with their arms are distracting and are making noise which stops him from sharing information. Their movements send the message they are not listening to Evan so he does not keep talking. The illustration (and other similar ones to follow) was designed to communicate the idea of Evan's words being interrupted by the characters' *actions*.

Page 12

Not only does Ellie feel uncomfortable with the actions of some of the children in the group, so do the flamingos! They do not like all the extra movement and noise. Note: In all illustrations, the animals communicate thoughts and feelings too!

Page 13

Now that the kids are listening with their whole bodies, the flamingos are feeling comfortable again.

Page 16

Notice that even though Molly is *not* talking, she is trying to direct the kids' attention to the monkeys. Their moving hands make Molly think they are not paying attention to her.

Page 18

How are Evan and Jesse feeling? How do you know? What clues do you see on their faces and bodies? How are Molly and Ellie feeling? How do you know? Discuss the idea that when we are not using whole body listening, others can feel differently than we do at that moment.

For example, Ellie and Molly are feeling happy but are not listening. This makes Evan and Jesse feel mad because Ellie and Molly are not connected to what is going on around them.

Page 19

Now how are Jesse and Evan feeling? Have their thoughts and feelings changed? How do you know? How are Ellie and Molly feeling? They changed what they were doing and now they are connected to the group. That makes everyone happy.

Page 27

Discuss the positive results of listening with their whole bodies. When they listen with their whole bodies they can think with their eyes and follow the zookeeper's plan. Now the group can have some fun and feed the giraffes.

Structured Activities

After you have completed the story and corresponding Teaching Moments, the following activities are used to reinforce the Social Thinking concept. Keep in mind that your purpose is to model the use of the vocabulary as much as possible during teachable moments.

Draw attention to times when your students are listening with their whole bodies. It is important to use the vocabulary at the time you notice children doing the concepts well, so students can pay attention to what they are expected to do. If the vocabulary is used to tell children what not to do ("See Pearl, she is not listening with her whole body."), then students pair the words with bad behavior and not as a tool through which they can learn positive lessons.

"Listen With All of You" Music Activity

- Cue track 6 on the CD: "Listen With All Of You."
- Preview the song to familiarize yourself with the language used. (Find lyrics in Appendix B.)
- Act out lyrics with children as you listen together!

Make Your Whole Body Listen!

Use the Body Part Cards from Lesson 1 (in Appendix A and on materials CD) to practice making different body parts not listen (by making them move around) and then making them listen.

Start out by mixing up the body part cards face down and selecting a few, one at a time, for the entire group to practice. If you draw the hands card, for example, the entire group can start to wiggle their hands and fingers, wave them around, clap them, even just fidget around or tap them on the table. Once everyone is moving that body part ("Oh no, our hands aren't listening!") you'll have to figure out how to make them listen ("To make our hands listen we have to stop moving them!"). A countdown to help kids get their hands quieted can be helpful here, especially because a license to wiggle can get students wound up. Once the group has stopped, tell them that now their whole bodies are listening again. Repeat with a few more body parts. Make a point to talk about which students are using whole body listening really well.

Once the group has had lots of practice moving together, each person in the group can take a turn selecting a card then making that part of his or her body move. Engage the group to help the child figure out how to make his or her body listen again. For example, "Oh no, Avery's mouth isn't listening! What can she do?"

Note: In addition to the individual body parts, there is also a whole body card to use. When this card is drawn, move your whole body, then make your whole body listen!

When your group is ready to make this a little more challenging, have one person draw a card and not show it to the rest of the group. The child whose turn it is then moves that body part and the rest of the group tries to guess what part of his or her body isn't listening.

Zoo Adventure/ Acting Out the Story

Turn your room into a pretend zoo as described in the preparation section of this lesson plan.

Keeping your bodies in the group, visit each animal and act out the story. Have the children first practice not listening with each body part that represents the animal. Observe students who are imitating well and tell them they are also doing a good job thinking with their eyes! Then cue children to stop and listen with that body part.

- Alligators: make arms move up and down like alligator jaws. Then verbally cue, "Now, listen with your arms!"
- Flamingos: stand on one leg. Then cue, "Now listen with your legs!"
- Chameleons: look all around the room. Then cue, "Now listen with your eyes. Think about me!"
- Monkeys: pretend to peel bananas. Then cue, "Now listen with your hands!"
- Cheetahs: run around the room or in place. Then cue, "Now listen with your feet!"
- Lion: make a big ROAR sound. Then cue, "Now listen with your mouth!"
- Elephants: pretend to make large elephant ears and flap hands by ears. Then cue, "Now listen with your ears!"
- Giraffes: it is time to put all the parts together. Cue, "When I see you listening with your whole body, I can tell you want a turn to feed the giraffe." Hand out paper leaves to children when they are demonstrating whole body listening. Each takes a turn putting a leaf in the giraffe's mouth.

Dramatic Play: Reinforcing the Concept and Vocabulary

Prepare Materials for Dramatic Play

- Gather images related to a trip to the zoo to use as your children talk, brainstorm and plan.
- Copy template 2, Lesson 5 (Appendix A) that contains individual images of things found at the zoo: a flamingo, an alligator, a giraffe, a monkey, an ice cream stand, and the zoo keeper. Cut out/enlarge images and have them handy to attach to your thought bubble prop.
- Locate props to be used in recreating any of the ideas you or the children generate about going to the zoo. Some props may overlap with previous activities. Some suggestions include:
  - Stuffed animals or images of zoo animals
  - Blocks
  - Binoculars
  - Tickets made of paper
  - Bus (ride to the zoo)
  - Picnic supplies (blanket, play food)
  - Map of zoo

A Trip to the Zoo

Using the Social Thinking concept and vocabulary during less structured playtime is a perfect opportunity to help children learn to use the vocabulary with their peers and appreciate that whole body listening is an important aspect of being around others.

Set Up

Begin by telling students, "In our group we read the story about going to the zoo. Today we are going to pretend to make a trip ourselves. Let's think about the zoo. What do we know?" You can use the story to help provide context and items found at the zoo (find template in Appendix A and on the materials CD). Consider the following to help your group think about the zoo:

- How can we get to the zoo?
- What might we do at the zoo?
- What animals would we see there?

As the children brainstorm, place pictures of items in the thought bubble. For example, if Mabel shares that we can see monkeys at the zoo, place a picture of a monkey in the thought bubble. If a child shares an idea that is not pictured, feel free to draw a quick sketch to visually represent the idea.

Verbally cue students: "Together we thought about the zoo and all the different things we can see and do. Now let's make a group plan. What should we do on our zoo adventure?"

Listen to your students brainstorm ideas for play. Suggestions for ideas might include:
- Build a zoo together – decide which animals will go where and make each habitat.
- Assign roles (animals, zookeepers, visitors, ticket takers) and pretend to play zoo.
- Picnic at the zoo.
- Pretend to bring an animal home from the zoo. What might happen if an elephant lived in your house?

Once the group has brainstormed ideas, it is time to make a play plan. You will go in one of the following directions with your group:
- Teacher chooses activities and everyone follows that plan.
- Take turns following each child's plan.
- Students put their ideas together to make a group plan.*

*   Please remember, **some groups may not reach collaborative play for a long time!**

The goal of the playtime is to illustrate the vocabulary in action. Model the use of whole body listening in the context of going to the zoo and related activities. Use the following examples as a guide to facilitating play.

Use the body part cards to provide visual feedback while you talk with children. Remind them of the different body parts that need to listen, not just one's ears!

"Courtney is listening with her eyes, ears, hands, and feet." (Show cards for a visual as you highlight the listening body parts.)

"Sarah, make your hands listen please." (Show "hands" card.)

The final part of play is always clean up! Continue to use the vocabulary during this time. Examples include:
- "Listen with your whole body – it's time to put the toys away."
- "Marjorie is saying she needs help! Brenna is listening with her whole body to hear how she can help."
- "Paul, show Randi you are listening with your whole body."

Beyond the Lesson: Generalize the Vocabulary to Other Settings

Just because the lesson is over doesn't mean the learning stops! Continue to use and reinforce the vocabulary in future lessons and throughout your time together with students. Some suggestions follow.

Your students may also find two books related to the whole body listening concept enjoyable: *Whole Body Listening Larry at School* and *Whole Body Listening Larry at Home*, both by Elizabeth Sautter and Kris Wilson and available at www.socialthinking.com.

While getting ready for circle time:
- "I can tell Anais is listening with her whole body. Her feet are quiet, her hands are resting in her lap, her mouth is not talking, and her eyes are looking at and thinking about me! She is ready for circle time."
- "Stephanie, make your hands and feet listen. Show me you are ready for circle time."
- "Caden, make your whole body listen."

Choice Time:
- "Chloe is listening to Lucie with her whole body."
- "Ricardo, listen with your whole body. Amy is showing you what she wants to play with."
- "Mykel, Heath is trying to tell you his idea. Show him you are listening with your whole body."

When group time is ending:
- "Jenny and Alex are showing me they are listening with their whole bodies. They look ready to go home."
- "If your mouths aren't listening, you won't be able to hear your name!"
- "Listen with your whole body for the plan."

Take Away Points for This Lesson

On the following page you will find a list of the key core concepts we want students to take away from this lesson. Review the list and assess your student's knowledge based on the rubric below.

0 =	No understanding of the concept. They are not using the vocabulary or demonstrating any of the requisite associated behaviors.
1 =	Emerging awareness of the concept. May be able to point out or give examples of its use or misuse on others but are not demonstrating its use even with maximum support and cuing.
2 =	Emerging awareness of the concept. May be able to point out or give examples of its use or misuse on others and are demonstrating its use with support and cuing.
3 =	Solid understanding of the concept and can demonstrate its use with moderate cues.
4 =	Solid understanding of the concept and may be starting to use it with minimal cues.
5 =	Solid understanding of the concept and can demonstrate its use with minimal cues.

If you rate a student at 0 on the majority of the bullet points, consider:
The appropriateness of curriculum for this student. (See page 36 in introduction.)

If you rate a student at 1 or 2 on the majority of the bullet points, consider:
Spending more time teaching this concept before moving on to the next lesson. Explore it in different ways and across settings.

If you rate a student at 3 or above on the majority of the bullet points, consider:
Continuing to use the concept in context and teachable moments as you move forward in teaching the next lesson or deepening knowledge on this one.

Lesson **5** Take Away Points for *Whole Body Listening*

The expectation is for kids to be exposed to (not master) the following concepts:

- Listening involves all of your body, not just your ears!

- We use whole body listening to make our brains available to take in all the information around us (what the eyes see, the ears hear, etc.).

- We use whole body listening to show other people we are listening but also to figure out what is going on.

The Family Letter: Extend Learning Outside the Classroom

As children learn new Social Thinking vocabulary, it is helpful to solicit the help of parents and family members in using the same vocabulary at home.

Find the Family Letter in Appendix C and on the materials CD in the back of this book.

Lesson **5**

Whole Body Listening

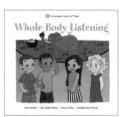

Family Letter and At Home Activities

In our Social Thinking group today we learned about the concept of **whole body listening** (Truesdale, 1990).

Whole body listening is when your eyes, ears, mouth, hands, arms, legs, and feet are calm and quiet. When you listen with your whole body it helps you pay attention to what people are doing around you and it shows others you are thinking about them.

Exploring this concept helps increase our awareness of how we listen when we are part of a group as well as the nonverbal messages we are sending when others are talking with and to us. Listening with our whole bodies, and subsequently focusing on and thinking about the group, sets the stage for successful communication and interaction.

In this adventure, Evan, Ellie, Jesse and Molly take a trip to the zoo. They learn that when all of their body parts are calm and quiet, it shows others they are thinking about them. When they listen with their whole bodies, they get to visit and learn about lots of animals, and everyone feels good about being together.

In this example, Ellie and Molly are not listening with their whole bodies.

Everyone is doing whole body listening. Even the Cheetah is happy now!

Lesson 5. Template 1. Whole Body Card

Lesson 5. Template 2. Items Found at the Zoo

Appendix **A** **Templates**

Appendix **B** **Song Lyrics**

Appendix **C** **Family Letters**

Appendix **D** **Ideas for Goal Writing**

Lesson 1. Template 1. Thought Bubble for Teacher

Lesson 1. Template 2. Thought Bubble for Students

Lesson 1. Template 3. Talking Bubble

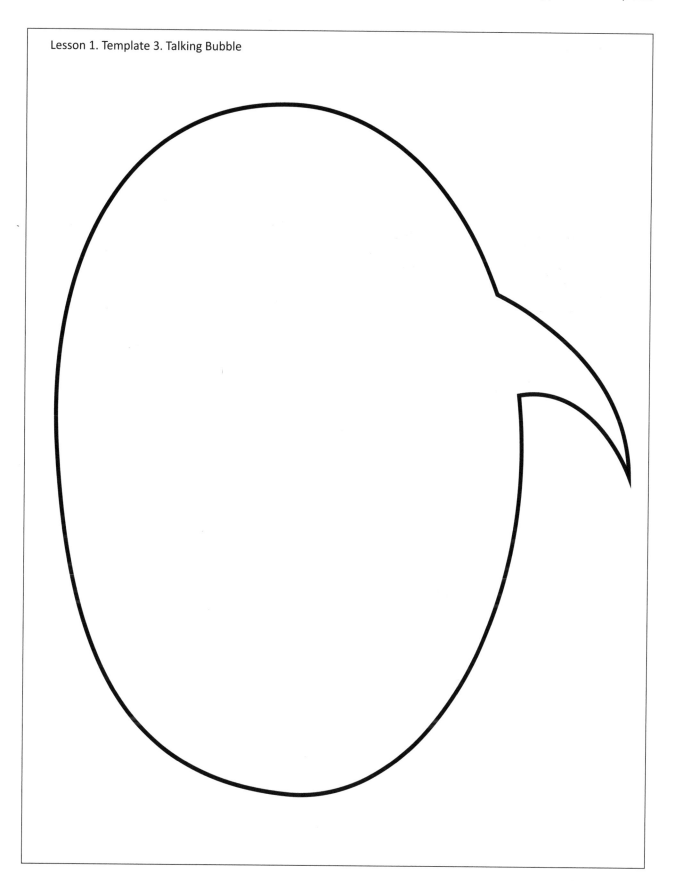

Lesson 1. Template 4. Body Part Cards
Images on template on CD are sized to fit on a 4" preschool block.

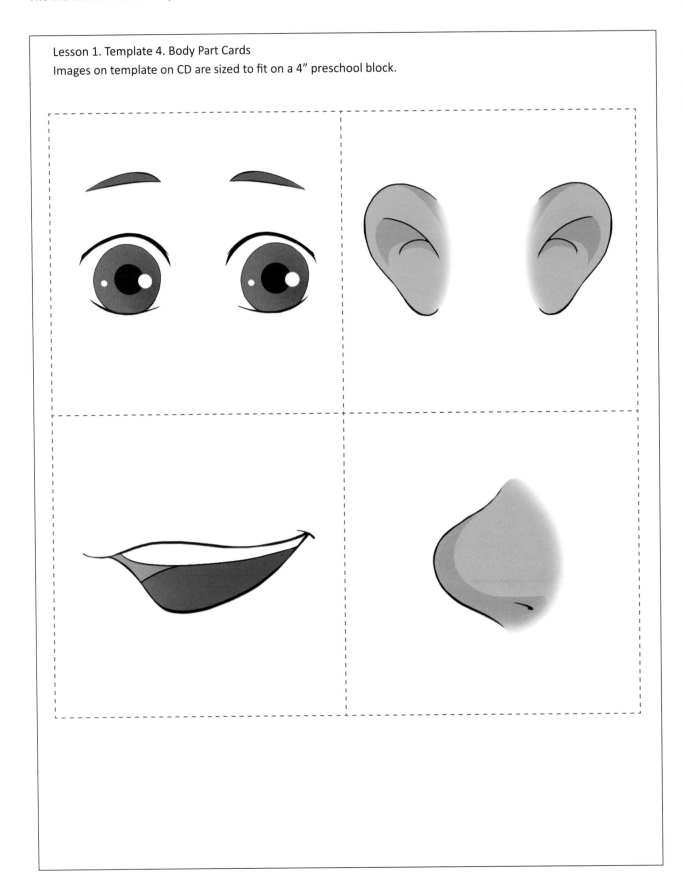

Lesson 1. Template 4. Body Part Cards
Images on template on CD are sized to fit on a 4" preschool block.

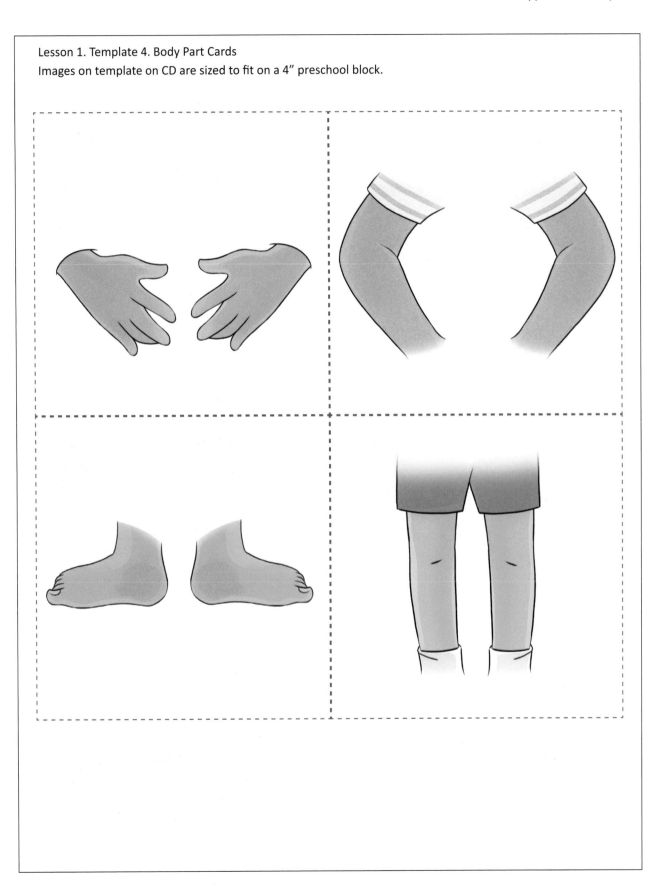

Lesson 2. Template 1. Apples

Lesson 2. Template 2. Items Found on a Farm

Lesson 3. Template 1. Items Found in Outer Space

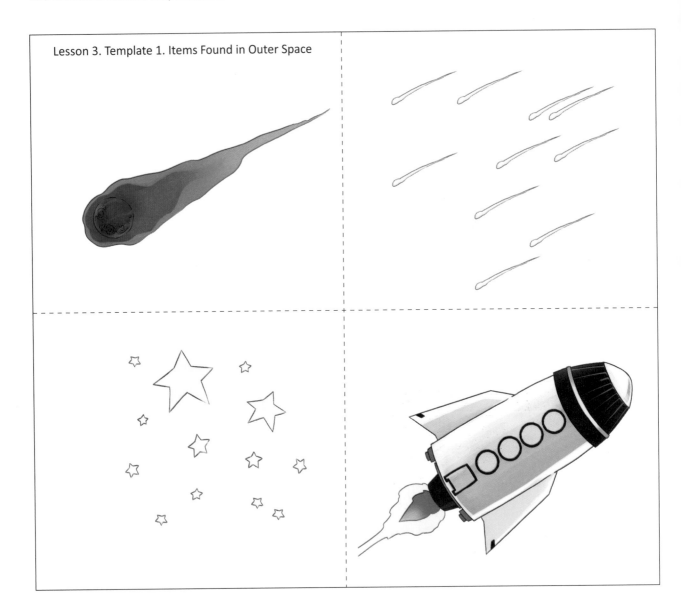

Lesson 3. Template 2. Aliens

Lesson 3. Template 3. Planets

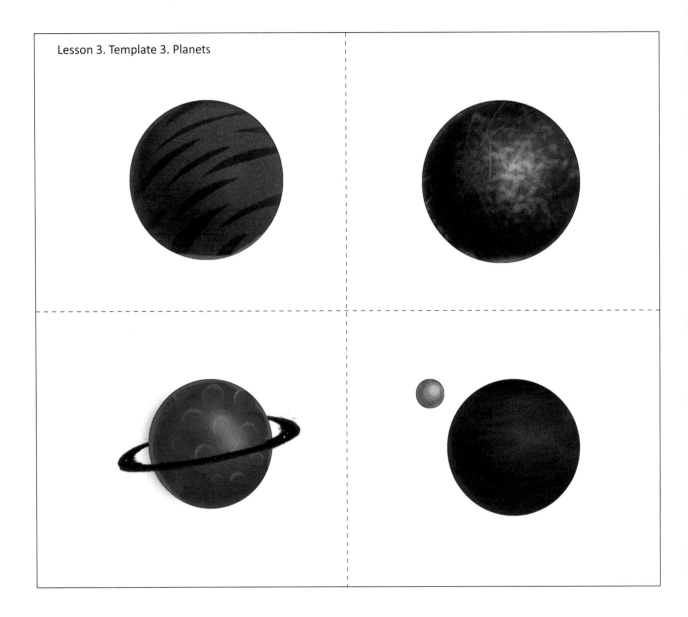

Lesson 4. Template 1. Items found in the Ocean

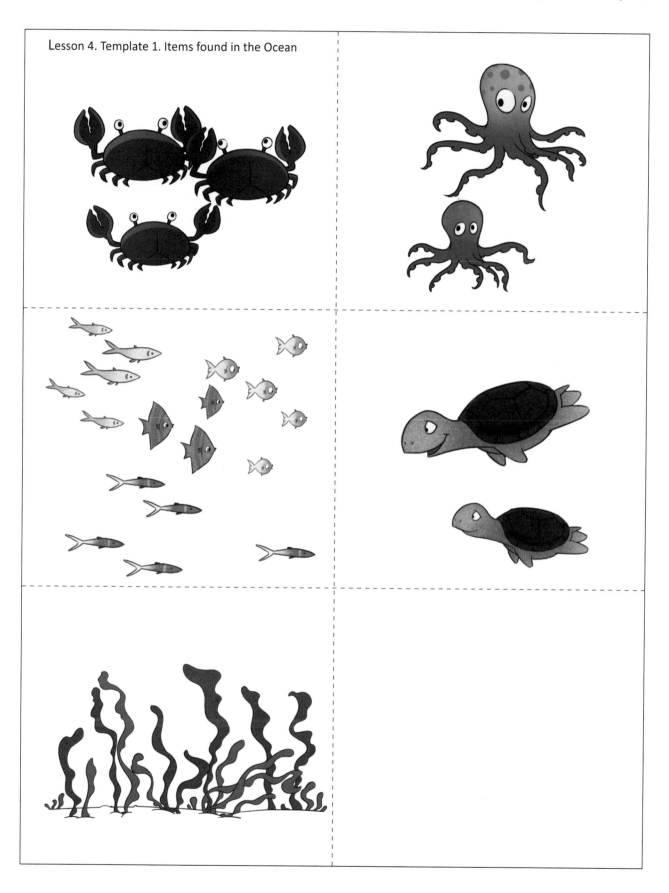

Lesson 4. Template 1. Items found in the Ocean

Lesson 5. Template 1. Whole Body Card

Lesson 5. Template 2. Items Found at the Zoo

The Plan Template

Where You
Think a Thought

Words and music by Tom Chapin & Phil Galdston

You got fingers to snap (snap snap), two hands to clap (clap clap)
Ten toes to tap (tap-a-tap-tap), but your brain is where you think a thought

You got legs to walk (left, right), a tongue to talk (blah, blah, blah, blah)
You can walk and squawk (squawk), but your brain is where you think a thought

You got a mouth to drink (slurp slurp), two eyes to blink (blink blink)
One place to think (ohhhhh) and your brain is where you think a thought

You got ears to hear (what?), whoever's near (who?)
Still it's very clear (Yessir!), that your brain is where you think a thought

It's like a picture there, it's underneath your hair, it's where you think
And thinking happens quick, it's like a magic trick, it's like shazaam!
When you think, when you think a thought
When you think, think, think a thought

Every day you grow, there's new stuff to know, new thoughts that flow
In your brain when you think a thought
If you think it through, it might occur to you that I'm thinkin', too
My brain is where I think a thought!

It's like a picture there, it's underneath your hair, it's where you think
And thinking happens quick, it's like a magic trick, it's like shazaam!
When you think, when you think a thought
When you think, think, think a thought

So go on and think (ohhhhh) and if we think in sync (oh, oh)
We'll form a link (cool!) to the thoughts up in our brains
We got a nose to smell (sniff sniff), we got a story to tell, (blah, blah, blah, blah)
Now we know darn well (Yessir!) that our brain is where we think a thought
Our brain is where we think a thought
Our brain is where we think a thought

Where you think, where you think a thought
Where you think, think, think a thought

Show Me
What You're Feeling

Words and music by Tom Chapin & Phil Galdston

Well, it starts in the heart of every boy and girl
It flows through your veins, right to your brain
And goes out to the world
When you're happy, you're up and open
When you're sad, you're closing down
When you're scared, you're small and scrunched up
When you're excited, you jump around

So, laugh everybody, ha, ha, ha
Cry everybody, wah, wah, wah
Sing everybody, la, la, la
Shake your head, everybody, nah, nah, nah
Down to the ground, up to the ceiling
Let me know what you know
Show me what you're feeling
Show me what you're feeling

Well, it moves through your muscles, your elbow and your knee
And evry time you move, it only goes to prove
That you're a lot like me
When we're mad, our hands are clenched up
With our faces in a frown
When we're calm, we're loose and easy
We let whole wide world go 'round

So, laugh everybody, ha, ha, ha
Cry everybody, wah, wah, wah
Sing everybody, la, la, la
Shake your head, everybody, nah, nah, nah
Down to the ground, up to the ceiling
Let me know what you know
Show me what you're feeling
Show me what you're feeling

Everybody dance, everybody cheer
Let me see you grin from your ear to your ear
Everybody look, everybody see
If I smile at you, you'll smile at me

Show me what you're feeling

The Plan

Words and music by Tom Chapin & Phil Galdston

When it's you and only you
You're alone, all on your own
But when it's you and me and we
There must be a plan

When it's you and only you
It can be fun when you're just one
But when it's you and me and we
We can make a plan

That's the aim, that's the game
To find out all you can
Snoop a little, solve the riddle
And then you'll understand

That it's you and me and we
A special group that's in the loop
That's the place you want to be
It's fun to know the plan

It's so much better, working together
Sticking to the plan

Then it's you and me and we
A special troop that knows the scoop
Cause when the plan is plain to see
And we follow, you and me
That's the greatest place to be
Because you understand
And yes, you know you can
Be a big part of the plan

Think With Your Eyes

Words and music by Tom Chapin & Phil Galdston

Open your eyes, take a look, look real carefully
Is that a grin, over my chin?
Think with your eyes and see
It's all in one place, right here on my face,
and if you look at me
You might find a frown or a smile upside down
Think with your eyes, you'll see
Think with your eyes and see!

Your eyes can be a microscope, seeing close as close can be
Maybe I'm sad, maybe I'm glad
You can tell if you look at me
Your eyes can be a telescope, seeing far as far can see
If I'm happy, you'll know, if I'm not, it'll show
You can tell if you look at me

Open your eyes, take a look, look real carefully
There's many a clue of what you should do
Think with your eyes, you'll see
Think with your eyes and see

Your eyes can be a camera, keep a picture in your mind
Maybe I'm hot, maybe I'm not
You can tell almost every time
Your eyes can be a lighthouse, they can send a special sign
When you're looking at me, you're thinking of me
I can tell almost every time

So, open your eyes, take a look, look real carefully
Is that a grin, over my chin?
Think with your eyes and see
It's all in one place, right here on my face,
and if you look at me
You might find a frown or a smile upside down
Think with your eyes, you'll see
When you're looking at me, I know you're thinking of me
Think with your eyes and see!

In the Group

Words and music by Tom Chapin & Phil Galdston

If it's one, make it two, make it me and you
If it's two, make it three, you and you and me
If it's three, make it four, cause three could use one more
If it's four, make it five, bring this group alive

Everybody has a body
Keep your body in the group
We found our way in, now, let's stay in
Workin', playin' in the group

Make it seven, if it's six, do it just for kicks
If it's seven, make it eight, eight is always great
If it's eight, make it nine
Nine is really fine, if it's nine, make it ten
Then start it all again

Everybody has a body
Keep your body in the group
We found our way in, now, let's stay in
Workin', playin' in the group
Eyes and nose in, fingers, toes in
Knees and elbows in the group
Don't be strayin', let's just stay in
Workin', playin' in the group

One, two, three, four, five, six, seven, more
Eight, nine, ten, then, start all over again

Everybody has a body
Keep your body in the group
No delayin', when you're stayin'
Workin', playin' in the group
Eyes and nose in, fingers, toes in
Knees and elbows in the group
No complainin', keep your brain in
Keep your body, your whole body
Everybody in the group

Listen
With All Of You

Words and music by Tom Chapin & Phil Galdston

List'nin'...lookin'...stillin'...
Open...closin'...chillin'...

List'nin' with...lookin' with...stillin' both...
Open up...closin' up...chillin' with...

List'nin' with your...lookin' with your...stillin' both your...
Open up your...closin' up your...chillin' with your...

List'nin' with your ears, lookin' with your eyes, stillin' both your feet
Open up your brain, closin' up your mouth, chillin' with your bottom on a seat
List'nin' with your ears, lookin' with your eyes, stillin' both your feet
Open up your brain, closin' up your mouth, chillin' with your bottom on a seat

Use your whole body, use your whole body
From your head to your toe, using everything you know
Listen with all of you

List'nin' with your ears, lookin' with your eyes, stillin' both your feet
Open up your brain, closin' up your mouth, chillin' with your bottom on a seat
Use your whole body, use your whole body
From your head to your toe, using everything you know
Listen with all of you

Listen...ears, lookin'...eyes
Still both your feet
Open up...brain, closin' up...mouth
Chill...with your bottom on a seat
Listen with your ears, eyes, brain and mouth, while you're
Stillin' both your feet
Listen with your ears, eyes, brain and mouth, while you're
Chillin' with your bottom on a seat

Use your whole body, use your whole body
From your foot to your shin, from your knee to your thigh
From your belly to your chest, from your chin to your eye
From the way down low, to the way up high
Listen with all of you

My Own Detective

Words and music by Tom Chapin & Phil Galdston

Looking for the how to's
Hunting down the good news
There are lots of clues that I can learn
Some are don'ts and some are do's
Don't get angry when I lose
Do let others always take their turn

Gonna be my own detective
Evidence? I will collect it
Every tip, yeah, I'll inspect it, somehow
If I want to stay connected
Gotta track down what's expected
And be my own detective, now

I found out a new fact
When I look, they look back
How I act is all that they can see
So, I use my cool detective tools
To investigate the rules
Now, I can tell what they expect of me

Gonn be my own detective
Evidence? I will collect it
Every tip, yeah, I'll inspect it, somehow
If I want to stay connected
Gotta track down what's expected
And be my own detective, now

Now, when they smile, I can smile
We're connected, you see
Now, when they change, I can change
It's the detective in me

Gonna be my own detective
Evidence? I will collect it
Every tip, yeah, I'll inspect it, somehow
If I want to stay connected
Gotta track down what's expected
And track down what's expected
And be my own detective
I'm gonna stay connected...now!

Look, Think, Guess, Know

Words and music by Tom Chapin & Phil Galdston

When everybody sits down and they all gather' round
Can you guess what I'm thinking? It's Circle Time
When the teacher has a book and she's asking you to look
Can you think what I'm guessing? It's Story Time
First, you take a good long look
And then you think it through
And if you make a real good guess
Maybe you'll know
Maybe you'll know

Look, think, guess, go
Mighty good chance you're gonna know
If you look, think, guess, go
There's a mighty good chance you'll know

When we gather up the blocks and we throw 'em in a box
Can you guess what I'm thinking? It's Cleanup Time
When I'm putting on a coat, put a scarf around my throat
Can you think what I'm guessing? It's Leaving Time
First, you take a good long look
And then you think it through
And if you make a real good guess
Maybe you'll know
I bet you'll know, yes!

Look, think, guess, go
Mighty good chance you're gonna know
If you look, think, guess, go
There's a mighty good chance you'll
Look, think, guess, go
Mighty good chance you're gonna know
If you look, think, guess, go
There's a mighty good chance
Look, think, guess, go
You'll know, I bet you'll know
Look, think, guess, go
There's a mighty good chance
There's a mighty good chance you'll know!

The Incredible, Flexible You

Words and music by Tom Chapin & Phil Galdston

When you've got your own plan
And you don't think you can
Do what the group wants to do
No need to pout, it's easy to work out
For the incredible, flexible you

You can twist, you can turn
You can change, you can learn
It's fun to be a part of a team, it's true!
When there's a surprise, it's a chance to exercise
The incredible, flexible who?
The incredible, flexible you

When you move a little from your plan
You can join with everyone
When you join with everyone you can
Have a lot more fun

When it seems like you're stuck
You're not, you're in luck!
Cause now you know what you can do
Take a moment or two and say hello to the new
Incredible, flexible who?
The incredible, flexible you

When you move a little from your plan
You can join with everyone
When you join with everyone you can
Have a lot of fun

When you've got your own plan
And you don't think you can
Do what your friends want to do
Who knows it's no prob? It's just another job
Who makes no fuss? Who can make a smart adjustment?
Who knows how it's done? Who has more fun?
Than the incredible, flexible
Incredible, flexible......you!

Size of the Problem

Words and music by Tom Chapin & Phil Galdston

Every day, stuff gets in my way
But I'll be ok 'cause I've learned to say
What's the size of the problem?

And when I know, no need to let my troubles grow
I know where to go and those who know
What to do to solve 'em

It it's small as a mouse, I can fix it myself
If it's big as a house, I can go ask for help
If it's worrying me, there are places to turn, once I learn
To recognize the size of the problem

How big, how short, how tall?
How big, how small, how short, how tall?
How big, how small, how short, how tall?
How big, how short, how tall?

If it's small as a flea, I can fix it myself
If it's big as a tree, I will need someone else
If it's worrying me, there are places to turn, once I learn
The size of the problem

How big, how short, how tall?
How big, how small, how short, how tall?

I'll be ok when stuff gets in my way
Because I've learned to say every day
What's the size of the problem?

How big, how short, how tall?
How big, how small, how short, how tall?

I Know You Know
(Imagination)

Words and music by Tom Chapin & Phil Galdston

I know, I know that you know
I imagine, you imagine
I know, I know that you know
If you pretend and I pretend it's one, fun
Imagination

You be a shark, I'll be a whale
Under the sea together
We can be clowns, clowning around
Every night in the circus together
All we've got to do is know that

I know, I know that you know
I imagine, you imagine
I know, I know that you know
If you pretend and I pretend it's one, fun
Imagination

I think some things, you think some things
Some things we think together
I play a game, you play a game
But it's best when we're playing together
All we've got to do is know that

We're fighting a fire, aiming the hose
Up on a ladder together
Or two astronauts, way out in space
Exploring the planets together
All we've got to do is know that

I know, I know that you know
I imagine, you imagine
I know, I know that you know
If you pretend and I pretend it's one, fun, imagination
One, fun
Imagination

You Can Bend

Words and music by Tom Chapin & Phil Galdston

You can bend like a bow when you know how to bend
You can bend like a knee when you need to
You can go with the flow when you know that you must
And trust it'll be okay

You can bounce like a ball when you know how to bounce
You can turn right around when you need to
You can roll like a wheel 'cause you know you can deal
And feel it'll be okay

If something strange comes your way, you can change, it's okay
and say to each new surprise...

I can bend like a bow 'cause I know how to bend
I can bend like a knee when I need to
I can go with the flow when I know that I must
And trust i'll be okay

When something strange comes my way, any time, any day
I can say to each new surprise...

I will bounce like a ball 'cause I know how to bounce
I can turn right around when I need to
I can roll like a wheel 'cause I know I can deal
And feel it'll be okay

We can bend like a bow 'cause we know how to bend
We can bend like a knee when we need to
We can go with the flow when we know that we must
And trust it'll be okay

Family Letter
The Incredible Flexible You™ Social Thinking Curriculum

Dear Families,

Welcome to *The Incredible Flexible You*, a Social Thinking® Curriculum for the Preschool and Early Elementary Years! Your child is beginning an exciting adventure in learning more about the social world. This letter is designed to introduce you to the curriculum and provide information about supporting your child's learning at home.

The aim of *The Incredible Flexible You* lessons is to help young verbal learners develop the skills they need to be flexible social thinkers and social problem solvers. Through the experiences of four characters in the storybooks and the accompanying lessons and music CD, children will learn about the social mind and social expectations. They will also learn about their own thinking (and that of others) to help them make better decisions when in the midst of social play and interaction.

The curriculum is based on Social Thinking, a treatment framework developed by Michelle Garcia Winner that teaches the "why" behind our social behavior. Winner created the Social Thinking Vocabulary and concepts as a way to break down, explain, and put into concrete terms the abstract concepts that make up our social world.

The Incredible Flexible You curriculum is divided into ten lessons that align with the ten storybooks in this teaching series. Each lesson is designed to teach a specific Social Thinking concept via one of the vocabulary terms. You will be receiving family letters that explain the concept as it is introduced in the curriculum and how to support your child's learning at home.

As you embark on this social learning adventure together, please keep in mind the following points:

- Social learning is slow and deep! We do not expect children to master concepts quickly.
- Learn about the concepts your child is being exposed to and start to use the same vocabulary at home. Talk about the concepts when you are at home, at the store, in the car – anywhere and everywhere! The more you can make the vocabulary part of your everyday language, the better.
- Complete the "At Home Activities" included in each family letter.
- Be sure to enjoy the stories and songs that accompany the lessons. They're designed for the entire family.
- Don't forget to notice and mention when your child is being a good social thinker (positive reinforcement!) and keeping other people feeling good about being around him/her!

Please note that the curriculum is designed for children with listening and language skills strong enough to understand and discuss the concepts presented in the storybooks. While all children will benefit from exploring these lessons, students with special learning needs may need much more time to do so.

We hope you and your family will have fun while learning and practicing these all-important concepts.

Lesson

Thinking Thoughts and Feeling Feelings

Family Letter and At Home Activities

Social learning is all about **thoughts** and **feelings.** The ability to think about others, play collaboratively and establish friendships is all about thoughts; knowing our own, sharing them with others and taking others' thoughts into account as we act and react. We introduce these concepts first because all subsequent concepts and vocabulary lessons are tied back to thoughts. (What are you thinking? What am I thinking? What is the group thinking about?) We make the connection to feelings because what we think and what we feel are inseparable.

In exploring thoughts and feelings, we begin by establishing a connection to body parts. Children are familiar with their bodies and we are able to use what they know: that we all have many body parts and each part has a job to do. In most cases, we can see these parts and watch them do their jobs. For example, we can see hands clap, hold, and touch, and feet tap, jump and run. We then connect that information to the more abstract concepts of thoughts and emotions. That is, there are other parts inside our bodies that have important jobs too. Our brain and heart are two of those parts we use when we are around people. Our brain is our thought maker. We define a thought as an idea, picture, or words you have in your brain. To help us talk about thoughts we use words like *think* and *know*. Our heart is our feelings keeper. A feeling is something we feel in our body. To help us talk about our feelings we use words like *happy, sad, mad,* and *scared.*

In the first story of The Incredible Flexible You™ series, we meet the main characters, Evan, Ellie, Jesse and Molly. These four children go on many adventures to introduce and explore Social Thinking Vocabulary and concepts. In their first adventure, they learn all about two important concepts: thoughts and feelings.

At home, it is important to raise your child's awareness that s/he is having thoughts. We practiced this by drawing attention to examples that were big and exaggerated. When children saw us do something unexpected (out of the ordinary, silly, etc.) we labeled the process by saying, "You are having a thought! I'm putting shoes on my hands, that's silly! You're having a thought about me."

You can continue to reinforce this at home by doing anything that's out of the ordinary or breaks the normal routine and labeling that process by saying "You're having a thought." Some suggestions include:

While getting dressed:
- Put socks on your hands. "You're having a thought. I put socks on my hands. That's silly. You're having a thought about me."
- Put pants on your head.
- Put a shirt on inside out or backwards.
- When leaving the house:
  - Carry something out of the ordinary to the door with you, such as the toaster. "You're having a thought. I'm taking the toaster to work with me. That's silly. The toaster stays in the kitchen. You're having a thought about me."
  - Put on a robe instead of a jacket, or slippers instead of shoes.

While the above activity exaggerates times your child would have a thought, it's important to remember we're always having thoughts, about things big and small. Contrast these over-exaggerated examples with times we're having thoughts during the day that are not as obvious and more routine.

Some examples of day-to-day thoughts we might have are:
- "I like bananas. I'm thinking about eating my banana."
- "It's time for dinner. I'm thinking about cooking."
- "I'm thinking about putting on my shoes."
- "I'm thinking about reading you a book."

Things I Like to Think About...
The following activity is included so your child can relate to this concept on a personal level and explore his/her own thoughts.

Instructions: Use the thought bubble handout at the end of the letter. Have your child draw a picture of himself or herself (or use a photo) and place it under the thought bubble. Then fill the bubble with pictures or drawings of things your child likes to do, play with, eat, etc.

Feelings Book
Begin by stapling four pieces of paper together on the left side, into book form. At the top of each paper, write a feeling word. Start with these feelings: happy, mad, sad, and scared. Either draw a picture or take a photo of your child making that facial expression. Together, talk about times the child has felt and experienced that emotion. Draw a picture, use photos from magazines, or personal photos of these times and add them to the page. Do not expect your child to be able to come up with examples independently. You may decide to make the book and then fill in the examples across time. For example, after a birthday party you might add a picture on the "happy" page.

As your child begins to learn and identify more emotions, add pages to increase the child's emotional vocabulary. Examples may include:

Proud	Comfortable	Jealous
Disappointed	Uncomfortable	Tense
Frustrated	Curious	Surprised
Excited	Confused	Grumpy
Worried	Calm	Silly

Things I Like to Think About...

Lesson 2

The Group Plan

Family Letter and At Home Activities

In our Social Thinking group today we talked about the **group plan**. In our story, Evan, Ellie, Jesse and Molly take a trip to the farm to make an apple pie and ice cream. They learn the difference between following their *own plan* versus the *group plan*. When one person followed his/her own plan, the group could not accomplish their goal. When they worked together and followed the group plan everyone felt good and they ended up with delicious treats to share.

In our group we use illustrations to show everyone thinking about the group plan together versus a person who is thinking about his/her own plan. (See the illustration below.) We talk about "the plan" as a way to help children know what they are expected to think about and do when they are working in a group. When everyone is following the plan, we are all thinking about each other. When we all think about each other, everyone feels good.

Suggested ways to extend learning about the Group Plan at home:

- Talk about "the plan" and what you are thinking. For example, "My plan is to make a snack." "The plan is to go to the grocery store." "The plan is to get ready for bed! Time to brush our teeth; follow the plan."
- Talk about what each person can say and do so all share the same idea/plan. Consider the following examples: "I'm thinking of the plan to go to the grocery store. I'm getting my coat." "Sayida is thinking about the group plan. She is helping to set the table for dinner."
- Point out the times when you are all sharing one plan. Talk about how that makes you feel. For example, "We are following the plan to get ready to go to school. I put on my shoes. You put on your shoes too! That makes me feel happy. Now we're ready to go." Or use pictures and words.

Group plan/own plan illustration.

In the story, the group plan was to pick apples. Evan followed his own plan and pretended to drive a tractor.

Activity 1

At Home Activity: Following the Plan!

Anytime we do something together we are following a group plan. Reinforce the idea that children follow a plan when they are at home too, not just at school. At home a group plan might include cooking and eating dinner, folding laundry, raking leaves in the yard, going on a bicycle ride, or going to the grocery store. There is a connection between our behaviors and other people's emotions. When we follow a group plan, it makes other people feel happy and makes us feel good too!

Draw a picture or take a photograph of a time when you did something together during the week. Some ideas include: playing a game, making a snack, eating dinner, going to the grocery store, or even sorting laundry! Draw a thought bubble (use template from Lesson 1 Family Letter) and adhere the photograph or drawing into the bubble. Then draw yourselves in the boxes below the thought bubble to show you are thinking about the plan and activity. See the example below.

Lesson **3**

Thinking With Your Eyes

Family Letter and At Home Activities

In our Social Thinking group today we talked about **thinking with your eyes.** Expressively we use our eyes to show others what we are thinking about. We look at people to let them know we are thinking about *them*, listening to *them*, talking to *them*, and/or sharing an experience with *them*. Receptively we use our eyes to gather information about what other people are thinking about, what is happening around us and what might be someone else's plan.

In the story we read, Evan, Ellie, Jesse and Molly take a trip in a rocket ship to outer space. They meet curious aliens. As the story unfolds, the aliens and children try to communicate but don't speak the same language. The children have to learn to think with their eyes to figure out what the aliens are looking at, how that connects to what they are thinking about and therefore, what they are planning to do next.

We will be using the term thinking with your eyes instead of behavioral directives such as "look at me" or "use eye contact." When children are taught to think with their eyes they begin to understand that there is a purpose for observing others and the environment. When you think with your eyes you are engaging in an active process that helps you determine what others are thinking, how they are feeling, and subsequently how to respond. It is more than just "looking" at something. Thinking is involved!

What a person is looking at is often what he or she is thinking about. We can use what others are looking at to make a smart guess about what or whom they are thinking about. For example, if you are talking with a friend and he is looking at you this means he is thinking about you and what you are saying to him. If we are looking at something other than the person talking to us, like a picture on the wall, we are sending the message that we are thinking about the picture and not the person who is talking, since looking equals thinking.

Eyes are like arrows, they point to what someone is looking at and most likely thinking about!

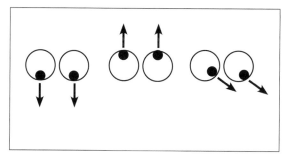

Activities to try at home

Activity 1
Cook something together and only use your eyes to think about the items you want or the ingredients you want to add. Make a cake, for example, and place all the ingredients out on the counter. Tell your child, "I am going to look and think about the ingredient I need." When it is time to add the eggs, look at your child and then look at the eggs. Verbally prompt your child, "Think with your eyes: what am I looking at, what am I thinking about?" If you've got more than one helper in the kitchen you can use your eyes to think about whose turn it is to add the ingredient.

Activity 2
Use everyday opportunities to ask for something around the room using only your eyes. For example, you might be getting ready to leave home and notice your car keys on a table. Tell your child "I need help before I leave! Think with your eyes. Can you figure out what I'm looking at and thinking about?" Maintain your gaze on the keys rather than shifting it back and forth between the child and the object so as not to confuse them.

Activity 3
Play a turn-taking game and indicate whose turn it is, based on who you are looking at (to show who you are thinking about).

Activity 4
When giving your child choices, ask him or her to look at the desired object. For example, at the dinner table hold the milk carton in one hand and juice in the other. Ask your child to think with his or her eyes, "Show me the one you want by looking at it." Then switch roles and have your child guess the drink you would like. Practice with everyone at the dinner table!

Activity 5
When you are reading books with your children, find opportunities to trace eye gaze and talk about what the character is looking at and thinking about. See the attached illustration from the book as an example.

Here, the kids are looking at space rocks and thinking about space rocks!

Lesson 4

Body in the Group

Family Letter and At Home Activities

In the *Body in the Group* story, Evan, Ellie, Jesse and Molly take a trip to the ocean. The group plan is to find a shark tooth and they quickly realize they need to think about each other and keep their bodies in a group to find it. When they keep their bodies in the group they finally find the shark tooth … and something they weren't expecting!

In our social thinking group we learned about the concept of **body in the group**. Keeping your body in the group means maintaining a comfortable physical presence around others – not too close, yet not too far away. When your body is in the group, it sends the nonverbal message that you are interested in others and that you are following the same plan. The opposite is also true. If your body is out of the group (too far away), it sends the message you are not thinking about the group. While we often realize the importance of language and what to say in a conversation, it is important to understand that physical proximity is also a key ingredient to successful social interactions.

Body in the group.

Body out of the group.

Activities to try at home

Activity 1 Use the body in the group vocabulary throughout your daily routines. Keep in mind that any time two people are sharing space, they are considered a group. Therefore, you can use the vocabulary when you and your child are alone, or when the family is together as a whole. Consider the following examples:

- "We can start our movie when all family members have their bodies in the group."
- "It's time for dinner. Everyone in the family has their body in the group, sitting at the table. We can start our meal together!"
- "When you leave the table, your body is out of the group. It makes me think you are finished with your meal."
- "Remember to keep your body in the group when we shop together at the grocery store."

Look through photo albums with your child. In the pictures, identify when people have their bodies in or out of a group.

 Watch for opportunities outside the home to observe others with their bodies in or out of groups. At a restaurant, for example, many people have their body in the group. Don't restrict yourself to groups of people either! One preschooler, for example, took a trip to the aquarium with her family. As they watched the schools of fish, she said "Look mom, that fish has its body out of the group."

 Music Activities

The Freeze

- Turn on some music and dance around. At random moments, pause the music and "FREEZE." Get the whole family involved.
- While "frozen" observe and discuss the physical presence of the people. Are you a group (about one arm's length away from each other) or is everyone all over the room? Whose body is still in the group? Who danced out? The object of the activity is not necessarily to stay in the group, but to observe and discuss what happened.

Hokey Pokey

Sing or listen to the "Hokey Pokey" together. In the song, each body part is placed in and out of the group! Sing and dance together while using the body in the group vocabulary.

Lesson 5

Whole Body Listening

Family Letter and At Home Activities

In our Social Thinking group today we learned about the concept of **whole body listening** (Truesdale, 1990).

Whole body listening is when your eyes, ears, mouth, hands, arms, legs, and feet are calm and quiet. When you listen with your whole body it helps you pay attention to what people are doing around you and it shows others you are thinking about them.

Exploring this concept helps increase our awareness of how we listen when we are part of a group as well as the nonverbal messages we are sending when others are talking with and to us. Listening with our whole bodies, and subsequently focusing on and thinking about the group, sets the stage for successful communication and interaction.

In this adventure, Evan, Ellie, Jesse and Molly take a trip to the zoo. They learn that when all of their body parts are calm and quiet, it shows others they are thinking about them. When they listen with their whole bodies, they get to visit and learn about lots of animals, and everyone feels good about being together.

In this example, Ellie and Molly are not listening with their whole bodies.

Everyone is doing whole body listening. Even the Cheetah is happy now!

Activities to try at home

Activity 1 Help your child get ready to listen with his/her whole body! Before you begin activities together, such as reading, use language to remind the child to turn on his/her listening body, one body part at a time (ears, eyes, arms, hands, belly, seat, legs, and feet). "It's time to listen with our eyes; that means you turn your eyes toward me." "It's time to listen with your hands; that means they are quiet in your lap."

Activity 2 Point out times your child is doing whole body listening. "I can see you're listening with your whole body. Your hands are listening, your feet are listening, your eyes are listening…" etc.

Activity 3 Help your child notice when s/he is not using whole body listening. "Oops, your eyes aren't listening! I can see you're looking at your toy when I expect you to think about me with your eyes!" Offer suggestions of what to do to use whole body listening. "Show me you're thinking about me and listening with your eyes. Now your eyes are looking at me, your hands are still and you are facing me. Now I know you're using whole body listening."

Activity 4 Play a game or put together a puzzle that involves body parts. Mr. Potato Head is a great example. Place the body parts into a bag or hide them in a bucket filled with dry rice or beans. Have fun finding the parts and placing them into the body. Talk about how Mr. Potato Head can show he is using whole body listening. Make a point of how hard this is for Mr. Potato Head to do since his body keeps falling apart!

Ideas for Goal Writing

At the end of each lesson it is important to take some time to think back through your students' social awareness and responses and assess their abilities in the areas covered by the lesson and those that follow. If you have gotten this far in the book, you may now realize, or you may already KNOW, that social thinking and social functioning is complex, multifaceted and multidimensional. We suggest the use of a rubric, as a goal with strict performance objectives does not lend itself to the type of flexible social thinking we are hoping to impart to our students.

The sample goals that follow are written with a rubric assessment format. It would not be possible for us to list every concept, skill, and behavior that can be targeted for treatment. Use these as a reference to help you organize your perceptions and observations to create accomplishable goals tailored to each individual child.

Concept: Understanding Self and Others

When provided with a photograph of himself/herself or others in a social scenario (e.g., playing with peers), student will identify his/her own and others' thoughts/feelings by demonstrating an increase of one point from baseline by _____ (date), as measured by the following rubric.

(Baseline: Rubric Rating = _____)

Note: this can be divided into two smaller objectives by separating the child's and others' thoughts/feelings into two parts.

Concept or Target	0	1	2	3
Thought/feelings- Understands self	Labels toys or children in photo with no mention of thoughts or feelings related to self	States at least one logical or plausible idea of what he/she might have been thinking	States at least one logical or plausible idea of what he/she might have been feeling	States at least one logical or plausible idea of what he/she might have been thinking and feeling
Thought/feelings- Understands others	Labels toys or children in photo with no mention of thoughts or feelings related to others	States at least one logical or plausible idea of what another might have been thinking	States at least one logical or plausible idea of what another might have been feeling	States at least one logical or plausible idea of what another might have been thinking and feeling

Concept: The Group Plan

1. Student will increase his/her ability (by _____ points above baseline) to identify what a group of people are doing (the group plan) during structured/unstructured activities as measured by the following rubric.

   (Baseline: Rubric Rating = _____)

   Note: goal/objective can be divided in two by splitting structured and unstructured, or both can be on the same rubric with 1 being more structured and 3 reflecting minimal support.

2. When directly asked, student will be able to distinguish between following one's own plan versus the group plan (score of at least 2) as measured by the following rubric:

Concept or Target	0	1	2	3
Understands Group Plan	Does not attend to others unless prompted to do so	Able to state the group plan when given **both** visual and verbal prompts (moderate support)	Able to state the group plan when given **either** visual or verbal prompts (minimal support)	Able to state the group plan when asked "What's the plan?"
Distinguishes Group Plan vs. Own plan	Does not understand concept	Can identify when someone else is following a group plan or his/her own plan	Can identify when he/she is following a group plan or his/her own plan	Able to state, draw, or otherwise show the concept of knowing about own plan versus group plan
Group Plan Follows a plan	Does not attend to others unless prompted to do so	Can follow a plan when given **both** visual and verbal prompts (moderate support)	Can follow the plan when given **either** visual or verbal prompts (minimal support)	Able to figure out and follow the group plan

Concept: Thinking with Your Eyes

1. Student will increase his/her ability to think with his/her eyes (by moving ___ points above baseline) to determine whose turn it is during a structured activity (e.g., a game) as measured by the following rubric:

    (Baseline: Rubric Rating = _____)

2. As measured by a rating of ___ across ___ sessions, student will increase his/her ability to think with his/her eyes by pointing out or giving examples of gaze direction in a static social scene (pictures, stop-action of video, or social scenario) in a structured setting.

Concept or Target	0	1	2	3
Eye Gaze Observing eye gaze of others	Does not attend to others unless prompted to do so	Able to point out gaze direction when given **both** visual and verbal prompts (moderate support)	Able to point out gaze direction when given **either** visual or verbal prompts (minimal support)	Able to point out gaze direction when asked, "What is he/she looking at?"
Eye Gaze Using eye gaze to make a choice	Does not understand concept	Able to direct his/her gaze to make a choice when given **both** visual and verbal prompts (moderate support)	Able to direct his/her gaze to make a choice when given **either** visual or verbal prompts (minimal support)	Able to direct his/her gaze to make a choice
(Older or more advanced student) **While observing the eye gaze and eye direction of others...**	Does not attend to others unless prompted to do so	Can figure out what another person might be planning to do when given **both** visual and verbal prompts (moderate support)	Can figure out what another person might be planning to do when given **either** visual or verbal prompts (minimal support)	Can figure out what another person might be planning to do

Concept: Body in the Group

1. When provided a photograph or video of him/herself or others in a social scenario (e.g., playing with peers), the student will identify whether his/her or others' bodies are in or out of the group, demonstrating an increase of 1 point from baseline by _____(date) as measured by the following rubric.

   (Baseline: Rubric Rating = _____)

   Note: goal/objective can be divided into two by addressing structured and unstructured separately, or both can be on the same rubric with 1 being more structured and 3 reflecting less structure.

Concept or Target	0	1	2	3
Observing others' bodies in the group	Does not attend to others unless prompted to do so	Able to point out when a peer's body is in the group when given **both** visual and verbal prompts (moderate support)	Able to point out when a peer's body is in the group when given **either** visual or verbal prompts (minimal support)	Able to point out when a peer's body is in the group when asked, "Which children have their bodies in the group?"
Observing own body in the group	Does not self monitor unless prompted to do so	Able to point out when his/her body is in the group when given **both** visual and verbal prompts (moderate support)	Able to point out when his/her body is in the group when given **either** visual or verbal prompts (minimal support)	Able to point out when his/her body is in the group

2. The student will increase his/her ability to maintain a comfortable physical presence (not too close and not too far) around others as indicated by an increase of 1 point from baseline by _____ (date) as measured by the following rubric.

   (Baseline: Rubric Rating = _____)

Concept or Target	0	1	2	3
Keeping one's body in the group	Does not attend to others unless prompted to do so	Able to keep his/her body at a comfortable distance from others in the group when given **both** visual and verbal prompts (moderate support)	Able to keep his/her body at a comfortable distance from others in the group when given **either** visual or verbal prompts (minimal support)	Able to keep his/her body at a comfortable distance from others in the group

Concept: Whole Body Listening

1. While observing other students in a variety of classroom activities (e.g. circle time, game, table work), the student will be able to point out the use of whole body listening, demonstrating an increase of 1 point from baseline by _____(date) as measured by the following rubric.

   (Baseline: Rubric Rating = _____)

2. While observing other students in a structured/unstructured activity, the student will be able to point out the use of whole body listening, demonstrating an increase of 1 point from baseline by _____(date) as measured by the following rubric.

   (Baseline: Rubric Rating = _____)

   Note: goal/objective can be divided into two by addressing structured and unstructured separately, or both can be on the same rubric with 1 being more structured and 3 reflecting minimal structure.

3. While observing him/herself in a variety of classroom activities (e.g. circle time, game, table work), the student will be able to display whole body listening, demonstrating an increase of 1 point from baseline by _____(date) as measured by the following rubric.

   (Baseline: Rubric Rating = _____)

Concept or Target	0	1	2	3
Observing whole body listening in others	Does not attend to others unless prompted to do so	While observing other students in a variety of activities the student will be able to point out the use of whole body listening when given **both** visual and verbal prompts (moderate support)	While observing other students in a variety of activities the student will be able to point out the use of whole body listening when given **either** visual or verbal prompts (minimal support)	While observing other students in a variety of activities the student will be able to point out the use of whole body listening when asked, "Are they listening with their whole bodies?"
Using whole body listening	Does not self monitor	Demonstrates use of whole body listening when given **both** visual and verbal prompts (moderate support)	Demonstrates use of whole body listening when given **either** visual or verbal prompts (minimal support)	Demonstrates use of whole body listening

Bibliography

Baron-Cohen, S. (2001). Theory of mind in normal development and autism. *Prisme, 34,* 174-183.

Beck, I. L., McKeown, M. G., & Omanson, R. C. (1987). The effects and uses of diverse vocabulary instructional techniques. *The Nature of Vocabulary Acquisition,* 147-163.

Behne, T., Carpenter, M., Call, J., & Tomasello, M. (2005). Unwilling versus unable: Infants' understanding of intentional action. *Developmental Psychology, 41*(2), 328-37.

Bloom, L. (1998). Language development and emotional expression. *Pediatrics, 102*(5), e1272.

Bodrova, E. Leong, D.J. (1996). *Tools of the mind: The Vygotskian approach to early childhood education.* Englewood Cliffs, NJ: Merrill/Prentice Hall.

Carpenter, M., Call, J., & Tomasello, M. (2005). Twelve- and 18-month-olds copy actions in terms of goals. *Developmental Science, 8*(1), F13-20.

Carpenter, M., Nagell, K., & Tomasello, M. (1998). Social cognition, joint attention, and communicative competence from 9 to 15 months of age. *Monographs of the Society for Research in Child Development, 63* (4, Serial No. 255).

Choi, D. H., & Kim, J. (2003). Practicing social skills training for young children with low peer acceptance: A cognitive-social learning model. *Early Childhood Education Journal, 31*(1), 41-46.

Crooke, P. J., Hendrix, R. E., & Rachman, J. Y. (2008). Brief report: Measuring the effectiveness of teaching social thinking to children with Asperger syndrome (AS) and high functioning autism (HFA). *Journal of Autism and Developmental Disorders, 38*(3), 581-91.

Farroni, T., Csibra, G., Simion, F., & Johnson, M. H. (2002). Eye contact detection in humans from birth. *Proceedings of the National Academy of Sciences of the United States of America, 99*(14), 9602-5.

Gilliam, W. S. (2005). *Prekindergarteners left behind: Expulsion rates in state prekindergarten systems.* Foundation for Child Development *Policy Brief Series 3.* New York, NY: Foundation for Child Development.

Greene, R.W. (1998; 2001; 2005). *The Explosive Child: A New Approach for Understanding and Parenting Easily Frustrated, Chronically Inflexible Children.* New York: Harper Collins.

Harris, P. L., Kavanaugh, R. D., Dowson, L. (1997). The depiction of imaginary transformations: Early comprehension of a symbolic function. *Cognitive Development,* Volume 12, Issue 1.

Kupyers, L. (2011). *The Zones of Regulation.* San Jose, CA: Think Social Publishing, Inc.

Leslie, A. M. (1994). Pretending and believing: Issues in the theory of ToMM. *Cognition, 50*(1-3), 211-38.

Liebal, K, Colombi, C., Rogers, S. J., Warneken, F., & Tomasello, M. (2008). Helping and cooperation in children with autism. *Journal of Autism and Developmental Disorders, 38*(2), 224-38.

Meltzoff, A. N. (2005). Imitation and other minds: The "Like Me" hypothesis. In S. Hurley and N. Chater (Eds.), *Perspectives on Imitation: From Neuroscience to Social Science* (Vol. 2, pp. 55-77). Cambridge, MA: MIT Press.

Meltzoff, A. N., & Brooks, R. (2007). Eyes wide shut: The importance of eyes in infant gaze following and understanding other minds. In R. Flom, K. Lee, & D. Muir (Eds.), *Gaze following: Its development and significance* (pp. 217-2n). Mahwah, NJ: Erlbaum.

Meltzoff, A. N., & Brooks, R. (2009). Social cognition and language: The role of gaze following in early word learning. In J. Colombo, P. McCardle, & L. Freund (Eds.), *Infant pathways to language: Methods, models, and research directions* (pp. 169-194). New York: Psychology Press/Taylor Francis.

Meltzoff, A. N., & Decety, J. (2003). What imitation tells us about social cognition: A rapprochement between developmental psychology and cognitive neuroscience. *Philosophical Transactions of the Royal Society of London. Series B, Biological Sciences, 358*(1431), 491-500.

Miller, E. and Almon, J. (2009). *Crisis in the Kindergarten: Why Children Need to Play in School.* College Park, MD: Alliance for Childhood.

Prizant, B. M., Wetherby, A. M., Rubin, E., Laurent, A, C., and Rydell, P. J. (2006). *THE SCERTS® Model: Volume I Assessment; Volume II Program planning and intervention.* Baltimore, MD: Brookes Publishing.

Rapacholi, B.M., and Gopnick, A. (1997). Early reasoning about desires: evidence from 14-18 month olds. *Developmental Psychology, 33*, 12-21.

Sautter, E., & Wilson, K. (2011). *Whole Body Listening Larry at School!* San Jose, CA: Think Social Publishing, Inc.

Segal, M. (2004). The roots and fruits of pretending. In E. Zigler, D. Singer, & S. Bishop-Josef (Eds.), *Children' Play: The roots of reading* (pp. 33-48). London, UK: Zero to Three Press.

Shonkoff, J. P., & Phillips, D. A. (Eds.) (2000). *From Neurons to Neighborhoods: The Science Of Early Childhood Development.* Washington, DC: National Academy Press.

Slaughter, V., Dennis, M. J., & Pritchard, M. (2002). Theory of mind and peer acceptance in preschool children. *British Journal of Developmental Psychology, 20*(4), 545-564.

Tomasello, M. (1995). Joint attention as social cognition. In C. Moore, P.J. Dunham (Eds.), *Joint attention: Its origins and role in development* (pp. 103-130). Hillsdale, NJ, England: Lawrence Erlbaum Associates, Inc.

Tomasello, M. (2009). *Why We Cooperate*. Cambridge, MA: MIT Press.

Tomasello, M., Carpenter, M., Call, J., Behne, T., & Moll, H. (2005). Understanding and sharing intentions: The origins of cultural cognition. *Behavioral and Brain Sciences, 28*(5), 675-735.

Truesdale, S. P. (1990). Whole-body listening: Developing active auditory skills. *Language Speech and Hearing Services in School, 21*: 183-184.

Vermeulen, P. (2012). *Autism as Context Blindness*. Overland Park, KS: AAPC Publishing.

Warneken, F., & Tomasello, M. (2008). Extrinsic rewards undermine altruistic tendencies in 20-month-olds. *Developmental Psychology, 44*(6), 1785-8.

Wilson, K., and Sautter, E. (2011). *Whole Body Listening Larry at Home!* San Jose, CA: Think Social Publishing, Inc.

Wimmer, H., & Perner, J. (1983). Beliefs about beliefs: Representation and constraining function of wrong beliefs in young children's understanding of deception. *Cognition, 13* (1): 103–128.

Winner, M.G. (2005). *Think Social! A Social Thinking Curriculum for School-Age Students*. San Jose, CA: Think Social Publishing, Inc.

Winner, M.G. (2007). *Thinking About YOU Thinking About ME*. San Jose, CA: Think Social Publishing, Inc.

Vygotsky, L. S. (1966). Play and its role in the mental development of the child. *Soviet Psychology, 5:* 6-18.

About the Authors

Ryan Hendrix, MS, CCC-SLP is a Social Cognitive Therapist at Social Thinking Stevens Creek in San Jose and a private therapist in San Francisco. Her diverse caseload experience includes preschool-age children through young adults with varying levels of social cognitive learning challenges. In addition to running groups, she actively collaborates with families and professionals (teachers, resource specialists, psychologists, etc.) on ways to promote carryover and generalization of learning outside the clinic setting. Ryan also helps supervise and train graduate students and clinicians in their clinical fellowship year and does ongoing mentorships within the Social Thinking Stevens Creek clinic.

Ryan's artistic and creative talents allow her to present lessons in a visual, fun, and engaging manner. Working with a variety of ages and levels allows Ryan to sit on the floor, fly around in a cape and create Superflex tools, then turn around and explore the concept of a clique or break down the hidden rules of hanging out at a café. She is passionate about Social Thinking and enjoys collaborating with students, families, and their teams to take Social Thinking beyond the clinic walls.

Kari Zweber Palmer, MA, CCC-SLP, started her career as a speech language pathologist in the public schools in Minnetonka, MN, working predominately in early childhood with some time at the elementary level. She provided assessment and intervention to children with a variety communication disorders including: autism spectrum disorders, apraxia, phonological, fluency, and voice disorders. She worked as a full time therapist at Michelle Garcia Winner's Center for Social Thinking in San Jose, CA. Her diverse caseload included preschool aged children to young adults, all with varying levels of social cognitive challenges. Kari had the good fortune of training directly with Michelle for two years before the Palmer family relocated back home to Minnesota.

Currently Kari works at her private practice, *Changing Perspectives,* in Excelsior, MN. She is a Social Thinking consultant in the Minnetonka Public Schools, and works with dedicated educators across the district (early childhood through high school) on implementing social cognitive teaching into the school day. Kari is an active presenter and likes nothing better than to share the power of Social Thinking with others.

Nancy Tarshis, MA, MS, CCC-SLP is a speech-language pathologist whose prolific career includes extensive experience working with children and their parents. In 1992, she joined the professional team at the Children's Evaluation and Rehabilitation Center (CERC) at Albert Einstein College of Medicine, where, in 1996, she was named Supervisor of Speech and Language Services. Currently, she maintains a clinical practice, seeing patients birth to 21 for diagnosis and therapeutic treatment, supervises ten speech pathologists, lectures to medical residents and psychology interns, participates in research projects, and serves as adjunct clinical instructor at Teachers College, Columbia, Hunter College, NYU, and Hofstra University. She is deeply experienced in a wide variety of treatment methodologies, including Social Thinking, and is a frequent speaker across the U.S. on its concepts and strategies.

Nancy's clinical work includes Altogether Social, a Social Thinking practice she co-founded with Debbie Meringolo that serves clients age 14 months through 22 years. Altogether Social provides individual and group sessions, consultations to public and private schools, and trainings for parents and professionals.

Michelle Garcia Winner, MA, CCC-SLP is a speech-language pathologist who specializes in the treatment of students with social cognitive challenges at the Social Thinking Center, her clinic in San Jose, California. She coined the term "Social Thinking" in the mid-1990s and continues to evolve the Social Thinking framework that today includes information, vocabulary, curriculum, and strategies that help children and adults around the world become better social thinkers.

The heart of Michelle's work is illuminating the often elusive and intangible world of Social Thinking, and developing practical strategies that can be easily used by parents, educators, and service providers across different environments. Her approach led GreatSchools.org, a leading national nonprofit organization, to call Michelle, "...the leading expert in the field of social skills." In 2008, she was awarded a Certificate of Special Congressional Recognition for developing this treatment approach.

Michelle is internationally recognized as a thoughtful and prolific writer, having authored or co-authored more than 20 books on Social Thinking. She travels internationally speaking on a multitude of topics relating to social learning, and repeatedly receives accolades for her educational, energetic, and enthusiastic presentations. Stephen Borgman at *Psychology Today* called her "… one of my favorite authors in the field of teaching emotional intelligence.

Social Thinking books, curriculum, worksheets, and related products developed by Michelle Garcia Winner and Social Thinking Publishing

Core Books about the Social Thinking Model & Curriculum

Inside Out: What Makes a Person with Social Cognitive Deficits Tick?
Thinking About You Thinking About Me, 2nd Edition
Think Social! A Social Thinking Curriculum for School Age Students
Worksheets for Teaching Social Thinking and Related Skills
Social Behavior Mapping: Connecting Behavior,
Emotions and Consequences Across the Day *

For School-Age Children

You Are a Social Detective! (co-authored by Pamela Crooke) **
Superflex... A Superhero Social Thinking Curriculum (co-authored by Stephanie Madrigal)
Superflex Takes on Rock Brain and the Team of Unthinkables By Stephanie Madrigal
Superflex Takes on Glassman (co-authored by Stephanie Madrigal)
Superflex Takes on Brain Eater (co-authored by Stephanie Madrigal)
Sticker Strategies: Practical Strategies to Encourage
Social Thinking and Organization, 2nd Edition
Whole Body Listening Larry at Home! By Kristen Wilson & Elizabeth Sautter
Whole Body Listening Larry at School! By Elizabeth Sautter & Kristen Wilson
We Can Make it Better! A Strategy to Motivate and Engage Young Learners in Social
Problem-Solving Through Flexible Stories By Elizabeth M. Delsandro
I Get It! Building Social Thinking and Reading
Comprehension Through Book Chats By Audra Jensen, M.Ed., BCBA
The Zones of Regulation: A Curriculum Designed to Foster Self-Regulation
and Emotional Control By Leah M. Kuypers, MA Ed., OTR/L
What is a Thought? (A Thought is a Lot) By Jack Pransky and Amy Kahofer
Movie Time Social Learning:
Using Movies to Teach Social Thinking and Social Understanding By Anna Vagin, PhD

* Available in English and Spanish   ** Available in English, French, and Spanish

Teens and Young Adults

*Socially Curious and Curiously Social: A Social Thinking Guidebook
for Teens and Young Adults* (co-authored by Pamela Crooke)
*Social Fortune or Social Fate: Watch Their Destiny Unfold
Based on the Choices They Make* (co-authored by Pamela Crooke)
*Social Thinking Worksheets for Tweens and Teens:
Learning to Read in Between the Social Lines
Social Thinking Across the Home and School Day
Strategies for Organization: Preparing for Homework and the Real World
Social Thinking at Work: Why Should I Care? A Guidebook for Understanding
and Navigating the Social Complexities of the Workplace* (co-authored by Pamela Crooke)
*Should I or Shouldn't I? A Game to Encourage Social Thinking and Social Problem Solving
Middle & High School Edition* By Dominque Baudry, MS., Ed.
*Movie Time Social Learning:
Using Movies to Teach Socal Thinking and Social Understanding* By Anna Vagin, PhD

Related Products

*You Are a Social Detective Interactive CD
Social Thinking Posters for the home and classroom
The Zones of Regulation Poster
Superflex Poster
Whole Body Listening Larry Poster*

Visit our website for more information on our books and products, free articles on Social
Thinking topics, and a listing of Social Thinking Conferences across the U.S.

www.socialthinking.com